DIGITAL MARKETING INSIGHTS 2018

ROI Driven Digital Marketing
Mumbai · Bengaluru · Chennai

Notion Press

Old No. 38, New No. 6
McNichols Road, Chetpet
Chennai - 600 031

First Published by Notion Press 2018
Copyright © Social Beat 2018
All Rights Reserved.

ISBN 978-1-64324-314-6

This book has been published with all efforts taken to make the material error-free after the consent of the author. However, the author and the publisher do not assume and hereby disclaim any liability to any party for any loss, damage, or disruption caused by errors or omissions, whether such errors or omissions result from negligence, accident, or any other cause.

No part of this book may be used, reproduced in any manner whatsoever without written permission from the author, except in the case of brief quotations embodied in critical articles and reviews.

Contents

Introduction .... *vii*

Did You Know

Digital Marketing Trends 2018

Digital Marketing Trends That Are Going to Die in
India in 2018 25

Social Media Trends for Real Estate in 2018 29

Google Case Study – How a Multilingual Approach
Got Us 90% Growth in Leads 34

Casagrand Generated a Record 190 Crores in Revenue
via Facebook 38

What Brands Can Learn from YouTube Brandcast 2018 40

Are Mobile Apps Close to Extinction? 46

What Can Brands Do to Engage with India's Next
Billion Internet Users 50

ऑनलाइन क्षेत्रीय कन्टेन्ट की बढ़ती 58

Marketing Mix Insights

Marketing for Companies: Time to Shift from Print to
Digital Media? 65

Sector Specific Solutions

The Ultimate Guide to Digital Marketing for the Financial Industry 71

How Digital Marketing Will Transform Real Estate Industry in 2018 79

How Digital Marketing for FMCG Brands Will Revolutionize the Sector... 90

5 Social Media Strategies to Boost Your E-Commerce Business.. 101

Social Media Marketing Insights

Guide to Using Facebook Live Effectively 109

The Ultimate Guide to Using Instagram Stories.................... 115

How to Use Pinterest for Your Brand 119

How to Use Instagram for Business: A Guide on Instagram Ads 123

Here Is Why You Should Use Linkedin in Your Marketing Plan 131

The Ultimate Guide on Brand Marketing via Snapchat........ 136

Advertising

The Ultimate Guide on How to Advertise on YouTube........ 143

The Most Definitive Guide to Optimize Your Adwords Campaign 151

UX & Web Design

How UX Can Break or Make Your Business Sales or Revenue 161

How Design Can Help Tell a Brand Story 170

Content Marketing and SEO

Content Marketing v/s Native Advertising 179

What Type of Content Will My Target Audience Find Engaging? 185

Content Amplification Strategies to Effectively Promote Your Content 199

How to Rank a One-Page Website 203

Ultimate Checklist for On-Page and Off-Page SEO 207

9 Ways to Leverage Local SEO and Google Maps for Your Business 217

Videos

How to Create Low Cost Videos to Tell Your Brand Story 225

App Marketing

A Beginner's Guide to App Marketing 231

App Store Optimization Cheat Sheet 235

About Social Beat *239*

Introduction

Digital marketing, over the years, has transformed into a dedicated marketing channel from being one of the supporting platforms in a company's marketing plan. Understanding the potential of going digital, companies are changing their marketing objectives from just brand awareness to lead generation and other such quantifiable techniques.

In fact, digital advertising spends in India has grown at around 30% in 2017 and this growth is expected to further increase in 2018. As one of India's leading digital marketing solutions company, Social Beat is happy to have been part of this phenomenal growth and to have leveraged digital media to drive results for our clients. Some of the business results achieved for our clients include:

- Over 1200 crore worth of sales for real estate clients across India, through integrated digital marketing efforts
- Engaged over 120 million Indians via social media campaigns for clients across Industries
- 4x increase in organic traffic using advanced Search Engine Optimization (SEO) and content marketing techniques
- Clients are achieving 55% of overall sales through digital marketing while spending only 25% of the marketing budget on digital campaigns.

This book deals with the different aspects of digital marketing and how this medium can be used to grow a brand and increase sales and revenue. Additionally, the book throws light on:

- Surprising statistics on how the nation is consuming digital content
- Sector-specific solutions: Real estate, BFSI, FMCG, e-commerce
- Brand building techniques: Content marketing and effective video marketing on YouTube and Facebook
- Performance marketing trends: ROI-driven strategies, platform-specific best practices and used cases

The book has been written and compiled by our team of digital marketing experts – Suneil Chawla, Vikas Chawla, Abhishek Kumar, Rohit Uttamchandani, Anuradha Nair, Purushothaman K, Panisa Shah, Farida Bharmal, Nandita Raman, Ayesha Rafeeq, Rhea Jain, Pournima Balasubramanian, Harshita Parikh, Vimal Michael, Rignesh H and Boobalakrishnan.

All the insights shared in this book would not be possible without the amazing support of our clients who have pushed us to achieve higher goals and constantly raise the bar. To all our clients – a big thank you.

We trust that you will find this compilation insightful. If you have any feedback or suggestions, we would love to hear from you at team@socialbeat.in. Happy reading!

Did You Know

Over 95% of videos consumed in India are not in English

Indian Internet users:
2017–450 million
2021–635.8 million

240 million users on WhatsApp and Facebook in India

80% of all Indians use their phones to access the Internet

28 percent of all searches are voice searches

Indian language Internet users will be more than 2.5 times of English users by 2021

Digital spending is expected to grow 2.5X from $40 billion to $100 billion

92% growth in searches for physical stores

53% of mobile users leave a page that takes longer than 3 sec to load

In 2018, 92% of marketers are expected to launch at least one influencer campaign

Digital Marketing Trends 2018

Digital Marketing Trends That Are Going to Die in India in 2018

With close to 450 million Indians already online, the digital industry is fast evolving. Since the launch of Jio, India has seen 9 times the growth in usage of Internet data. Owing to this, the dynamic platform of digital marketing has witnessed a lot of progression and development. The digital trends that worked a few years ago have reached their expiry date and newer trends that are more effective have emerged. Let us take a look at few of the digital marketing practices that are no longer effective in today's day and age and their improved versions that have taken over the online community.

Non-personalized emailers

Nobody likes mass emails that flood their inboxes with coupons and deals they are not interested in. Non-personalized emails are clearly dying out as the content may not be relevant to the audience you are sending it out to. Email marketing works when it is done right. Mass emailers have been upgraded with personalized emailers that are guaranteed to catch the audience's attention. Apart from mere personalization in the form of your potential customer's name, you can retarget them with what they were previously searching for and present them with irresistible offers based on their demographics, interests and past behavior on your website. This will not only pull them towards your website but will also leave them constantly refreshing their inbox in a quest for more deals and offers.

Quantity Over Quality

Brands have always been misguided by the notion that the higher the number of posts they put up on social media or the higher the number of blogs they upload on their website, the more traffic their content will generate. However, the truth is that with the abundance of content available online, it is more important to provide viewers with high-quality content that really stands out rather than a multitude of average blogs that will just get lost in an ocean of information.

The trend of bombarding your target group with a plethora of information until they ultimately get converted to loyal consumers is now a thing of the past. Potential customers are now being targeted with fewer posts comprising of content that the audience will find engaging. The secret lies in a primary purpose in the blogs, like showcasing a particular product, branding or luring viewers with an emotional connect. This strategy coupled with content amplification techniques will ensure that the content reaches the right target group.

Marketing on Twitter

Though Twitter is one of the leading social media platforms, the strategy of using Twitter as a marketing tool is on a decline. Though Twitter did post higher revenue for the last financial year, we are not seeing a significant growth in the user base in India. Brands are flocking to other effective mediums like Facebook, YouTube and Instagram, where they are more likely to get better reach due to the higher number of active users. Additionally, the cost of ROI and effectiveness of advertising spend on Twitter vis á vis the other platforms are very different. While Twitter does well in some genres like news, entertainment and politics, it is not a preferred platform for all brands in India.

Short-form Blog Content

Blogs are extremely important for any business. However, if you want to leverage the power of content marketing to showcase your brand and attract leads, it is time you bid adieu to short-form content. The average length of a blog is usually around 800 words, but in order to rank on Google, you need to work on longer content with in-depth analysis, research and loads of information. According to data, a well-researched content that is around 2000 words has a better chance of ranking on page one of Google search. Pack your blogs with different types of content from infographics and videos to statistical research and relatable memes. Apart from different forms of visuals, optimize your content with keywords and related keywords, while you sit back and relax as viewers flock to your website. Also, make sure you interlink your blogs well to provide readers with more related posts and keep them hooked to your website.

At the same time, apps like Inshorts are growing due to its byte-sized articles – brands may want to continue experimenting by using both short-form and long-form content depending on the purpose.

Manual Optimization of the Digital Ad Campaign

Optimizing your ad campaign is of key importance to generate leads and widen your client database. However, it is quite challenging and time-consuming to create a campaign and to manually check each digital ad campaign and optimize them as per industry standards. These practices are now being done using automated tools and artificial intelligence. For example, there are cost-effective tools like Optmyzr that allow automated optimization of advertising platforms like Google.

Relying on Organic Reach on Facebook

As dramatic as it may sound, there is no such thing as organic reach on Facebook anymore. As a brand, you need to promote your posts and invest in Facebook ads to reach your target audience. Facebook has also rolled out a new feature called "Explore Feed" tab, specifically for brands. This tab is a new feature on Facebook where users can view top relevant posts, which are handpicked for them based on their demographics, interests and content consumption.

Last-click Attribution

Last-click attribution is now being replaced by data-driven attribution. This upgraded trend is a process where the analytics model of the website credits the entire process of marketing, from attracting a potential buyer and procuring the lead to converting them to a consumer, rather than the last click that closed the sale. The last-click attribution model will let you understand that a recent buyer logged on to your website to indulge in a sale. But, the data-driven attribution model will give you a detailed insight of the consumer's journey, from the initial Google ad to the Facebook retargeting and emailer they received to push them to make the purchase.

Everything comes with an expiry date and digital marketing trends are no exception. It is time you upgrade your digital marketing strategies and stay ahead of the online curve.

Social Media Trends for Real Estate in 2018

Over the past few years, social media marketing has been one of the key marketing strategies for leading real estate developers to reach out to their potential buyers. For some developers, over one-third of their sales come from the digital medium. Advertising your property on social media platforms is a guaranteed way to showcase your property to real estate investors and increase the possibility of a sale. However, just posting images of your next upcoming project may not be captivating enough. Here are some new trends that real estate developers can leverage:

360-degree videos and photos

What if you could give your potential home buyers the luxury of a walkthrough of their new apartment without them leaving their homes? Sounds too good to be true? The latest trend of 360-videos will let you do just that. It is an excellent way to connect with your target audience and show the home buyer what is in store for them if they buy your apartment or villa.

While virtual reality is making an entry in the marketing scene, it is not mainstream yet because VR gear is expensive… However, if you are looking for an engaging video, then a 360-degree video is a good starting point. These videos can be created through low-cost tools as well.

This trend is highly beneficial in real estate for developers to showcase their upcoming projects. Apart from the 360-videos, developers can also use 360-degree photos to showcase an immersive 360-degree experience. Both the 360-videos and photos produce more engagement as well as message retention than regular videos or photos.

Casagrand, one of India's leading real estate developers, has used this marketing strategy to connect with their potential customers. For the launch of one of their projects in ECR, Chennai, they used 360-videos to exhibit what is in store for potential clients.

Growing importance of interactive ads

With organic reach on Facebook almost dead, brands are using focused advertising to reach their potential audience on social media. While the regular lead generation and website conversion ads are a great way to reach your target audience, it is also important to engage with the potential audience to understand them in order to improve the quality of your leads. A good way to do this is by using interactive ads. Interactive ads are the next generation of ads that have taken social media marketing by storm. These ads increase the engagement by interacting with potential customers. A typical example of an interactive ad is the Facebook live polls hosted by companies to produce user-generated data to study what the customers are interested in buying. For example, a real estate developer can put up a poll on Facebook to check if their clients prefer sea-facing apartments or pool-facing apartments. This will give them a rough insight into what their customers want and can even use this data in pricing their property.

If you are looking for the next level of interactive advertising, try out M-Canvas ads, a mobile-only advertising service with very interactive and engaging ad formats. They are unlike any other format available on social media. They are highly interactive and use a mix of images, videos as well as a carousel to create a memorable and stunning visual experience on mobile. Moreover, these ads allow you to interact within the publisher's domain i.e. while you are reading your news article on the same page you can interact with the ad, rather than going to a different page. Once you click it, the ads expand to give you further information and ensure the viewer interacts with the ad to take the next steps.

It is one of the best ways to showcase real estate products. For example, if your end goal is for your customer to enquire about the project, you can show a sneak preview of the project's interiors with a Call to Action that prompts viewers to take the next step. An audience, who is interested enough to swipe all the way through your ad is likely willing to click through to your website and make the enquiry. These canvas ads are a new concept that is catching up, and we see it as a trend that is here to stay.

Micro-targeting

Micro-targeting is a marketing strategy of using consumer data and demographics to identify the interests of specific individuals and then influence their action of making a purchase. If a property is for sale on OMR in Chennai or in Whitefield in Bangalore or BKC in Mumbai, with three bedrooms, three baths and is close to the IT corridor, then it is most likely to be bought by a working professional in his 30s with a family of two kids. With the help of micro-targeting, real estate developers can reach out to their target audience by specifying the demographics and the geography of the potential customer on Facebook. You can even target users around the world whose hometown matches the city where the project is. Hence, their ads are displayed to a more specific and niche crowd making the probability of selling the property even higher than before.

Growth of regional content and regional ads

Hindi content has been growing faster than English content and this is likely to increase even further in 2018. This is not only the case for content, but also advertising. If you are looking to reach a wider audience, especially in the Tier II and III cities, then using regional content is a must. Ads in regional languages have started rolling out and marketers have begun incorporating this concept into their marketing strategies to reach out to their target audience. When a potential home buyer reads an ad in his regional language, he develops a bond of trust and comfort with the seller and is more likely to make a purchase, or at least recommend that product to a friend.s

For example, Aryan Housing, one of the leading real estate developers based out of Mumbai, ran a campaign of ads in Marathi to connect with their local audience and received a phenomenal response.

Understanding this trend, Google has also recently started ads and keyword targeting in Indian languages to widen their reach.

Integrating offline and online marketing

While majority of first-time home buyers research online, they make the end decision of buying the property offline. So, for a real estate company, integrated offline and online marketing efforts are highly essential. While it is important to run ads and get leads, it is also important to understand that consumers do not make purchase decisions based on a single ad or message alone. Potential buyers gather all their information from various channels and this data gathered through several stages of the buying process are the building blocks of sales.

If you have a potential lead from an online ad and your sales team is following up with them, it is important to also reach out to that potential lead online as well. You could use automated email or drip email campaigns to reach them until they actually make the purchase. Real estate developers can target and constantly stay in touch with a group of people based on certain criteria. Let us say that a customer has visited a property website and shown interest by coming for a site visit, digital marketers can use the information provided by the customer to send emails about the development and completion of the property and news on various other related properties. Drip emails are a powerful lead nurturer, with statistics showing a 119% increase in click-through rate via trustworthy emails.

"Across the funnel" marketing

Advertising across social media platforms is all about building your brand and making it a household name for people to connect to and rely on. In "Across the Funnel" marketing, real estate developers build their brand names through four essential steps. They initially start the process by running engaging campaigns on social media, which explain their products and attract potential buyers. Then, they work towards increasing traffic to their websites and drive site visits and enquiries through their conversion data. Lastly, they customize their audience by eradicating cold leads and focus on customers, who have actively shown interest in their marketing campaigns. With Facebook's Brand Reach & Frequency campaigns, brands can even get assured visibility and reach, similar to what a front-page newspaper ad gives.

All of these social media marketing strategies are currently trending and are here to stay!

Google Case Study – How a Multilingual Approach Got Us 90% Growth in Leads

With the Indian real estate space getting increasingly crowded, it has become a significant challenge for developers to differentiate themselves from their competitors. In order to stand out, real estate developers need to try something unique to gain the upper hand. With the Tier II and Tier III cities being active on the Internet and most of them using the vernacular language to consume content, Casagrand formulated an innovative vernacular ad strategy to engage with India's next billion Internet users. Here is how Casagrand utilized vernacular content in their ads to reach this market and achieve an incredible 90% increase in leads.

The Objective

Casagrand Builders is one of the biggest real estate developers in South India, with a large presence in Chennai as well as projects in Bangalore and Coimbatore. They are committed to building aspirations and providing homes that offer families the highest quality and value. Casagrand had two main objectives:

1. To capture the mind space of potential buyers so they could stand out from their competitors.
2. To increase the number of leads, but drive down the Cost per Lead (CPL).

Sales Approach

In order to meet these objectives, we formulated a multi-targeted approach, which would capture the attention of potential buyers at various stages of the buying process. This would ensure that Casagrand would occupy a high position in the consumer's mind space and give it an edge over its competitors. To do this, we utilized three main strategies:

1. Localized Vernacular Ads

According to the Google and KPMG Report, the number of regional language speakers online in India will reach 76 million within the next five years. As this audience base grows in size and influence, it is important that brands start creating regional language content targeted towards them. Casagrand capitalized on this opportunity and developed a regional language-focused approach in their marketing strategy. We identified the Tamil-speaking consumers as the primary target audience, since most of Casagrand's projects are located in Chennai. Based on this, we began developing vernacular ads in Tamil, so we could reach out to these consumers directly. We used vernacular ads extensively for specific projects like Casagrand Uptown. Speaking to this regional audience in the language they were most comfortable with, Casagrand was able to develop a relationship built on trust and comfort with their target audience. This played a pivotal role in helping us generate high-quality leads for Casagrand.

2. Maximizing the Potential of Google Display Network

We identified the Google Display Network as the most effective way to reach our target audience to create maximum impact. Google Display Network allows us to find the right target audience and deliver our message contextually. One of the tools we used to maximize reach through custom affinity audiences. Building bucketed Custom Affinity Audiences allowed us to reach out to our specific target audience to ensure the right people were coming across our message. Gmail ads displayed at the top of a user's inbox also proved very effective in creating awareness and generating leads.

3. Leverage Brand and Generic Searches

One of the most important ways digital marketing is transforming the real estate sector is by creating brand awareness right from the initial stages of the buying process. As one of Casagrand primary objectives was to occupy the mind space of potential buyers, maintaining a high impression share across relevant keywords was very important. Through competitive bids on generic keywords (e.g. 2 BHK apartments in Chennai), as well as brand-specific keywords, we ensured that users would continuously come across Casagrand's ads in their search results. This helped increase the number of quality leads generated.

Results Achieved

Through this extensive and in-depth approach, we were able to generate an unprecedented increase in the number of leads for Casagrand. Our strategy of utilizing vernacular ads helped grow Casagrand 's leads by 90% QoQ and also increased the overall click volume by 85% QoQ. Vernacular ads were extensively utilized in the Casagrand Uptown project marketing strategy, with 50% of total spends being allocated to Indic Display Creative and targeting. This approach delivered significantly higher leads and a cost per lead (CPL) that was 60% lower than that of normal display creative. These results prove that vernacular ads offer massive benefits not just in terms of increasing brand awareness, but also in delivering higher ROI.

As the number of regional language users is growing at a faster pace than English language users, they are quickly becoming one of the most important segments for brands to focus on. The phenomenal results Casagrand achieved by implementing a strong vernacular ad strategy is proof that brands cannot afford to ignore India's regional audience.

Casagrand Generated a Record 190 Crores in Revenue via Facebook

Casagrand is one of India's fastest growing real estate companies and committed to building aspirations and delivering value. It offers superior homes in premium locations of Southern India. To date, the developer has delivered dream homes across 68 landmark properties to over 4,000 happy families.

We are delighted to announce that Facebook has published A Case Study on Casagrand's meteoric success, using Facebook marketing solutions. This is an important example of how no brand can risk ignoring the power of social media in today's digital landscape. In the last financial year, Casagrand, a real estate company based out of Chennai has generated an incredible 190 crores in revenue using Facebook marketing solutions and at a 60% lower CPL compared to other digital channels. Find out about how we helped our real estate client grow with real estate digital marketing for Facebook Marketing Solutions.

The Goal

Casagrand came to us with the objective of increasing their residential project sales through online enquiries and reducing their acquisition cost by 50%. To do this, we knew we had to devise a unique approach to Facebook marketing. We could not afford to use Facebook as just a brand-building tool, but also as a sales channel to boost residential sales. In all, we used eight Facebook marketing tools to generate record sales for our client through online enquiries alone. Each of these tools is crucial in brand building and lead generation.

How Did We Do It?

To help our client achieve their goals, the first thing we did was to run video ads on Facebook. Video is one of the key trends in social media to increase brand awareness and recall. Once we knew which of our target audience had viewed the videos, we were able to build a Custom Audience and target them again, using lead generation ads. These lead gen ads came with a pre-filled form with key information such as name, email and phone number, so all the potential customers had to do was click on the ad and enquire. Additionally, the builder also created lookalike audience of these leads and targeted them as well. The sales team too was quick to follow-up on these leads and convert them into buyers.

Using Facebook's reach and frequency tool, Casagrand pushed a specific offer to potential buyers for five days. This method increased both brand awareness and leads. To expand the reach beyond Facebook, the builder also used the audience network and Instagram platform to reach their target audience.

Using a combination on lead ads, slideshow ads and canvas ads, Casagrand was able to achieve their targets with real estate digital marketing using Facebook marketing solutions.

This case study is an important example of the power of social media marketing. With higher sales numbers and lower CPL, digital marketing has transformed the real estate industry.

What Brands Can Learn from YouTube Brandcast 2018

To mark its 10-year anniversary in India, YouTube hosted Brandcast 2018, an event to help marketers understand how Indians consume video content. Since it first launched in 2008, YouTube's rising popularity has been inextricably linked with India's own growth story, giving it a special understanding of the Indian Internet audience. Today, around 225 million Indians actively use YouTube every month just through their mobile phones. This number is set to increase to 500 million by the year 2020. With such a rapidly expanding audience base, YouTube is becoming increasingly more important for brands to effectively leverage. Interestingly, YouTube's reach is over 80% amongst the 55+ segment.

Brandcast 2018 provided invaluable insights into who is accessing YouTube, what content they are watching and how they are consuming it.

Opportunities for Brands on YouTube

YouTube has become one of the most important platforms for brands to engage with their consumers. The most remarkable feature of YouTube is that ads here have a very high reach and a *viewability* rate as high as 95%. The viewability rate refers to the number of audience members who have actually viewed the ad. YouTube's audience is one of the most engaged across all platforms and is also the best way to create a brand story. Brandcast 2018 revealed how actively users consume content on YouTube:

- 65% of YouTube viewers subscribe to their favorite channels while 85% of them watch newly uploaded videos within two days.
- 7 out of 10 viewers watch ads on YouTube with the sound on.
- More than 50% of female professionals watch YouTube videos for more information before making a purchase in categories like beauty, automobiles and real estate.

Clearly, YouTube can be extremely effective for brands to capture the attention of their audiences.

Case Study: On1y #ForkTheBananaLeaf Campaign

The use of creativity and engaging content works very well on YouTube since audiences are more inclined to spend a long time viewing your video. For the #ForkTheBananaLeaf campaign, On1y created a funny, unusual video to advertise their brand and to keep their viewers engaged. On1y is a premium spice brand with a signature grinder to ensure you get maximum flavor. They chose to speak about their product USP in an unusual way and effectively use humor to capture the attention of their audience.

The Concept

On1y wanted to steer away from the predictable storylines and advertise their product in a way that would increase brand recall among their audiences. To do this, they depicted a traditional South Indian wedding with the couple waiting to be served food on a banana leaf. However, instead of traditional South Indian food, they are served international dishes like pasta and pizza. While confused at first, they begin to love the food once they sprinkle seasonings by On1y over them. The idea of food with a twist was a unique play on the 'twist' of the grinder that is one of On1y's biggest USPs.

The Results

This video worked phenomenally well for Only and went viral in a very short time. The overall reach for the video was over 10,000,000, the total views on YouTube were over 480,000. Capitalizing on the huge success of the video, they also released a 'Behind the Scenes' video which also garnered a high number of views. This clearly showed that audiences were so engaged by the original video that they were willing to watch the second video about the same product.

Special Features on YouTube to Increase Brand Presence

YouTube has several different features and advertising options to help brands achieve their business goals.

Bumper Ads: 6-second videos, which can increase brand reach.

TrueView: In-stream ads, which play when a viewer is watching another video.

Video Ads Sequencing: A customized video funnel brands can create to take viewers through a journey.

Director's Mix: Make different versions of background copy on the same video based on various parameters of the target audience.

These tools allow brands to increase brand awareness, brand recall, physical store visits and ultimately, sales.

- Livon (Marico Industries) got a 7x conversion rate through the TrueView Ad format with 65% increase in modern trade and e-commerce.
- Duracell created a trust in power campaign and used 6-second bumper ads to complement their longer hero ads to increase brand awareness.

- Uber saw a 63% increase in first rides at an 18% lower cost/first trip after a YouTube Director's Mix campaign. Additionally, Australia's Campbell's Soup used the tool to generate customized creative for different audiences, leading to over 1.5 M total views and a 55% increase in Campbell's Simply Soup sales.
- Zain, a leading Saudi mobile and data services provider, achieved a 50% increase in brand search queries through video sequencing.

Influencer Marketing – A Growing Trend on YouTube

Influencer marketing has emerged as one of the most effective strategies brands can be used to build brand awareness and credibility. India has witnessed a growing number of powerful influencers in many different categories. Many of the biggest influencers today across all categories can be found on YouTube. From just 16 YouTube channels in India with over a million subscribers in 2014, there are now 300 channels. Indians today are using YouTube as a way to gain more information, rather than just for entertainment. They turn to YouTube influencers they trust to provide them with reviews, tips and tutorials. The Brandcast 2018 event revealed very important figures about how powerful influencers on YouTube really are.

- 7 out of 10 people relate to YouTube influencers more than celebrities
- 76% of businessmen who regularly consume video content say that YouTubers shape their perception of culture
- 65% of audiences who view videos have brand opinions, which have been strongly influenced by a YouTube influencer they follow
- More than 75% of moms' opinions on brands have been shaped by YouTube influencers

These numbers prove that YouTube is an indispensable platform for brands trying to widen their consumer base.

Rising Importance of Regional Content

The biggest avenue for growth is going to be regional audiences in Tier II and Tier III cities in India. While English-speaking audiences have almost peaked, regional language users online are only going to grow from here. Access to the affordable high-speed Internet as well as the availability of low-cost smartphones has made the Internet more accessible than ever before. Brandcast 2018 also revealed figures, which prove that regional content is going to become increasingly important for brands.

- 90% of time spent on digital videos in India is not in English.
- 60% of video content is consumed by cities outside the top 6 cities in India.

It has almost become a necessity for brands to explore regional language content in their marking strategy.

Case Study: Murugappa 'Update Azhagi'

At Social Beat, we have witnessed first-hand the power of regional content on YouTube. For the 'Good Netizen Good Citizen' campaign by the Murugappa Group, we conceptualized ideas for a video that would resonate with their audience base. As they are based out of Tamil Nadu, their target audience would be able to better understand and relate to Tamil language content.

The concept

The goal of the video was to effectively utilize humor to spread a message about responsible sharing on the Internet and to be a good 'netizen.' They created a funny yet thought-provoking series of videos on Internet etiquette. From a young woman who over-shares every mundane detail of her life with strangers to the way WhatsApp rumors are spread, these informative videos are aimed at raising social awareness on the responsible use of social media and the Internet.

The Results

These Tamil videos performed incredibly well on YouTube with one of the videos even getting over 570,000 views. Users also actively engaged with the video, leaving comments and sharing it on various social media platforms. Undoubtedly, the fact that the video was in Tamil played a very important role in the fact that it went viral.

According to the latest numbers, Tamil is currently the most used regional language in India among Internet users with 42%, while Hindi follows with 39%. Clearly, unless brands incorporate a strong regional language strategy in their marketing, they will be unable to engage with India's next billion Internet users.

YouTube is one of the biggest platforms for brands to reach out to their consumers. As its reach in India continues to grow, brands will need to learn how to effectively utilize it to grow their presence.

Are Mobile Apps Close to Extinction?

Digital technology has taken the world by storm. The labyrinth nature of the Internet has engulfed us with a blanket of convenience, making the world a much smaller place to live in. From booking a cab to ordering pizza, we have been spoilt for choice with the number of apps available in the market. Ever since the concept of applications was invented, these tiny widgets have evolved from the phone and tabs to laptops and even smart TVs.

In the past few years, there has been a drastic increase in the number of apps; however, the number of active app users has remained stagnant. According to a study, the average mobile app retention rate is just 20% after 90 days. Even if they have stayed on and not deleted the app, on an average, more than 75% of users fail to return the day after first use. These figures make us wonder – are mobile apps close to extinction?

While some of the essentials apps such as WhatsApp and Facebook will remain an active app on the phone, the rest of them will predominantly disappear. So, what is the future?

Progressive Web Apps – The future of apps

The newest trend observed on the Internet is the emergence of websites with app-like behavior in a browser. A shortcut to these websites can then directly be added to your device's home screen based on how frequently you visit them. The progressive functions of these app-like websites have coined the term **Progressive Web Apps,** which is the next big thing in the effervescent digital world.

Features of Progressive Web Apps

- A Progressive Web App integrates the experience of an app in a website, providing you with the best of both worlds.
- They look like normal websites that can be accessed from your browser. Based on your usage, the website will prompt you to add it as an icon on your home screen for direct access. With a direct shortcut, you can skip the process of visiting the website from your browser every time you log in.
- These websites are typically displayed in full-screen without a website frame, giving the user an app-like experience.
- With the progressive usage of these websites, you can experience full-fledged app behavior by granting permissions to access your device camera and contacts, as per the functions of the page.
- PWAs run on a JavaScript embedded with application shell architecture. These codes run in the background of the page and pre-load frequently visited images and information in the cache memory. This provides higher speed in loading the page with the combined benefit of easy offline usage.
- A PWA requires minimal page refreshes as it works like an app and not a conventional web page.

Advantages of PWAs

- A Progressive Web App eliminates the need to search for the native app in an app store and download it, consuming mobile data and time.

- It will send you notifications over time only after repeated usage, living up to its progressive nature.
- It loads very quickly, even in places of low connectivity, due to its exquisite application shell model.
- Contrary to native apps, it does not take up as much space on the phone. It just provides you with a shortcut to the website, which will behave like an app.
- It does not hamper your privacy settings or permissions. Even if it does, it will be over a span of time, based on your usage.
- The PWA does not need to be customized for iOS and Android platforms.
- It caters to feature-phones and entry-level smartphones that do not have enough space for multiple apps.
- While digital marketing is evolving in tier II and III Cities, 4G connectivity is still an alien concept. PWA is the perfect alternative to an app in tier II and Tier III.
- It also caters to the generation who are new to the Internet world for whom downloading an app is a tedious process.

How Can PWAs Benefit Brands?

Apart from the plethora of advantages an app user faces, a progressive web app can widely benefit any brand or organization. Gone are the days when websites were merely developed for desktop usage and apps for mobile phones. Considering the fact that most of the organic traffic comes through mobile, it is now mandatory for organizations to take their digital game up a notch to cater to their target audiences. A PWA fills in the gap between an app and a website and is the perfect solution for increased sales or leads.

Furthermore, the cutting-edge application shell architecture used in progressive web apps makes it ideal for e-commerce websites. It eradicates the need to download the app and provides the user with the added benefits of higher page loading speed and enhanced performance in places of limited connectivity.

Many leading organizations have already incorporated the concept of Progressive Web Apps in their digital space. Flipkart and Ola are a few of the early adopters of this technology. So, it's time for mobile apps to move on and welcome PWAs.

What Can Brands Do to Engage with India's Next Billion Internet Users

India is at a crucial moment in its digital story where it is slowly emerging as the most important internet audience in the world. While the global number of internet user growth has more or less peaked at around 10% annually, India's internet users grew by an incredible 28% up until 2016. Currently, there are about 450,000,000 internet users in India and going by current trends, 635.8 million Indians will be online by 2021. These developments offer both a unique opportunity and a challenge for brands. In order to make full use of the growing digital audience, brands need to find the best strategy to engage with the next billion internet users in India.

What are Indians Doing Online?

Indians are a sizeable presence across almost every major digital platform. Facebook is, by far, the most popular social media platform, with 240 million Indians users and most accessing it through their phones. These numbers prove that Facebook is a goldmine for brands looking to engage with their audience in the most impactful way. By effectively utilizing the top tools for social media analytics, brands can understand their consumers better and create more targeted campaigns.

There are currently 225 million Indians on YouTube, making it the second most used digital platform in India. This is significant, because YouTube ads can be a very effective way to attract and engage new consumers. There are also 50 million Instagram users in India, while there are 45 million Indians on LinkedIn. WhatsApp has quickly surpassed the previously used SMS as India's favorite text messaging service. 240 million Indians use WhatsApp daily to send around 50 billion messages globally. This points towards the use of WhatsApp for business becoming increasingly important for brands.

What Has Sparked This Growth?

While internet usage in India has been steadily growing over the years, there was a definite tipping point where the number of internet users in India exploded. There are two main catalysts for this development: the availability of low-cost smartphones and most significant of all, the launch of Reliance Jio. Jio started its services in September 2016 with a bang, offering its users free data. Even once the offer ended, the data plans for Jio remained much lower in comparison to other network providers. This sudden easy access to the internet led to India having the highest amount of data consumption in the world. Of the 150 crore GB consumed by Indians, 100 crore GB was consumed through the Jio network alone. What is perhaps the most exciting part is that Internet penetration currently stands at only 27%. This means that the number of Indians online is only going to grow from here, offering a huge advantage for brands.

How Can Brands Engage with These Consumers?

With India's internet audience growing by the minute, the stage is set for brands to tap into this huge market and engage with their consumers. Consumer engagement requires brands to realign their priorities from solely revenue-generation to actually creating value for their consumers. In India, brands can do this in a number of ways.

Understand Audiences to Personalize Marketing Strategies

In order to create content that consumers will actually find valuable, brands need to know who they're speaking to. By 2020, almost 40% of all internet users in India will be women. These points towards the growing importance of creating content that women will find relevant. Doing so will also involve challenging long-held assumptions with regards to gender and interest areas. For example, 60% of those who shopped for sporting goods and viewed related videos on YouTube were not men, but women. Additionally, 60% of those who searched for car-related information online were also women. Having an intimate understanding of audiences can help brands generate content that their users will actually find valuable. This is a crucial step in building a relationship with audiences.

Create Campaigns Specifically for Mobile

One of the most interesting characteristics of India's internet usage is that most Indians have not followed the general pattern of internet adoption. While globally, most people first used a computer and then migrated to mobile phones, Indians seem to have skipped the computer stage completely. According to a survey by Statcounter, Indians use their phones to access the internet almost 80% of the time. This means that brands should be producing content specifically designed for mobile phones if they want to engage the next billion internet consumers.

Use Regional Languages to Reach a Wider Audience

While the number of English-speaking internet users in India is largely static, the number of regional language users is growing at a breakneck pace. One of the key reasons for this growth is internet penetration in Tier II and III cities, along with villages. Digital marketing is constantly evolving in tier II and tier III cities and brands need to take note of this growth. In fact, Google estimates that about 30% of users in India are from rural areas. If brands want to develop a personal relationship with their consumers, then a strong regional language strategy is crucial. Tamil is the leading regional language used among internet users in India with 42% while 39% of users are Hindi-speaking.

Optimize Brands for Voice Search

Voice search in India might still be in the nascent stage at the moment, but it is growing at a steady rate. Google estimates that 28% of all searches are voice searches. Even more promising is the fact that there has been a 400% growth in Hindi voice search. Voice search has vast implications for SEO, because traditional keywords are not used when speaking naturally. For brands, this means that they have to find new ways to become discoverable through voice search results to stay visible on digital platforms.

Utilize the AdWords 'Missed Call' Extension

Adding call extensions to your ads can significantly increase click-through rates as well as conversion rates. But with a sizeable number of mobile users in India, especially in smaller cities and towns, using prepaid connections, the cost of making a call might stop them from contacting your business. This is why AdWords has recently rolled out a 'Missed Call' feature, which can help address this concern. When a user selects the Missed Call option on an ad, a call is placed and is then immediately cut. After this, the user will receive an automated call telling them to stay on the line while their call is connected to the business. During the same time, the business will also receive a call from Google. Once both the user and the business are on the call, they will be connected to each other. This feature can help brands engage with their consumers better as well as track conversions more effectively.

Encourage a Two-way Conversation

Digital marketing allows brands to not just speak to their consumers, but also to listen to them in return. This unique opportunity for a two-way conversation is crucial for building consumer engagement. To be able to have a meaningful conversation, brands need to understand exactly who their audience is, where their interests lie and what their concerns are. In the context of the current Indian audience trends, brands can only reach out to the next billion internet users once they look beyond the urban metros.

The Indian internet audience is more diverse than ever before. Only by gaining a deep understanding of India's unique audience can brands develop marketing strategies that will resonate with their consumers.

Growth of Regional Content Online

Every marketing expert knows the importance of content marketing. It is a great way to engage with customers and to provide them with knowledge. Creating content that is both engaging and relevant to the consumers is effective content marketing. With the growth of mobile and internet in India, every town and village in the country has access to the internet. Thanks to this internet revolution, most of the target audience can be found speaking in another language apart from English. So how are you going to address this problem? Our solution is a multilingual content strategy.

Hindi content consumption is growing at 94%

English is, of course, the most commonly used language online not just in the world, but also in India. However, according to Google data, there is a 94% growth rate in Hindi content consumption in the country. Keeping this in mind, global brands have started focusing on regional language as part of their strategy. A few years ago, Facebook users were flabbergasted to see the login page in Hindi script. US-based visual discovery tool Pinterest also launched a Hindi version, allowing users in India to try the translated version. Today, Google supports languages such as Hindi, Gujarati, Marathi, Bengali and Tamil, among others. With 234 million Internet users in India consuming content in local language, all global social media sites have realized the fact that if they do not go local in India, they might soon lose relevance. Understanding this phenomenon, Google is now focusing to expand usage of its products like Google Maps in vernacular languages, especially Hindi.

Regional content availability can boost the growth of internet in India by 24%

Of the literate 74% in India, only about 10% read English while the rest consume content in their vernacular language... According to the latest study conducted by the Internet, Mobile Association of India and IMRB International, regional content availability can boost the growth of the Internet in India by 24%. There are more than 70,000 newspapers printed in India and around 90% are printed in either Hindi or other vernacular languages. Realizing the importance of regional content, Indian app developers also understand the need for local app distribution platforms. International app stores currently do not allow the easy discovery of highly India-specific regional content.

Growth of regional language content: a case study

Yourstory.com, one of India's leading platforms for entrepreneurs, recently included separate sections for regional content to promote the entrepreneurial ecosystem.

The website also offers content in ten other languages including Marathi, Telugu and Bengali.

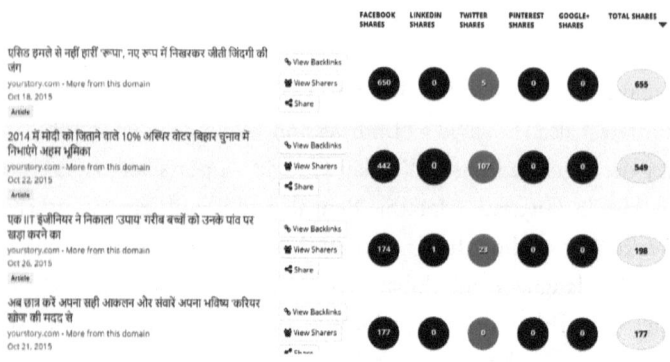

So, if you are convinced that regional content marketing is important, here are a few things to consider:

1. Wins audiences and drives traffic

It is easy to ignore other languages if one dominant language makes up the majority. While English does make for the majority, there is a section that only consumes content in a regional language and this section could be your most important target audience. An English creative gets 0.1% to 0.15% Click-Through Ratio (CTR), while a regional language creative can get 0.4–0.5% CTR. So, if a regional language content and creative can drive more traffic to your product or website, why not concentrate more on it?

2. Customers respond better to content in their mother tongue

When you market your brand in a regional language, it appeals to the emotional quotient of the audience. So, localization of content should be an integral part of the creation process. For instance, McDonald's, a leading food brand, includes its international teams at the beginning of product development stage, making sure they adapt a strategy that is in line with the country they are launching a product in. Their in-country localization teams ensure that the content stands out and strikes the right note in each country.

3. Integrate social media and content marketing

Your ultimate goal of participating in social media is likely to drive traffic to your website so you can convert those visitors into potential leads for your business. Without pitching brands directly, content marketing looks at generating relevant content that educates and creates awareness among customers. It has become an important marketing avenue for the fund-crunched start-ups to compete with the bigger brands. But, it is very important that your content is unique and engaging for your customers. Duplicate or low-quality content can prove to be counterproductive. Once your regional content is up and running, the next step is to ensure that it reaches your target audience. There are many content amplification techniques that can help you promote your content to a larger audience. The content strategy needs to be integrated with your social media marketing. Social media is the key to engaging with your potential and existing customer base as well as other brands and for marketing internationally.

ऑनलाइन क्षेत्रीय कन्टेन्ट की बढ़ती

हर मार्केटिंग विशेषज्ञ कन्टेन्ट मार्केटिंग के महत्व को जानता है। यह ग्राहकों से जुड़ने और उन्हें जानकारी प्रदान करने का एक बेहतरीन तरीका है। अपने लक्षित श्रोताओं के लिए प्रासंगिक और मूल्यवान कन्टेन्ट तैयार करना प्रभावी कन्टेन्ट मार्केटिंग का मूल है। भारत में मोबाइल और इंटरनेट की वृद्धि के साथ, भारत के प्रत्येक शहर और गांव में इंटरनेट तक पहुंच बन गई है। इस इंटरनेट क्रांति को धन्यवाद, ज्यादातर लक्षित श्रोता अंग्रेजी के अलावा अन्य भाषा बोलते हुए पाए जा सकते हैं। तो आप इस समस्या का समाधान कैसे करेंगे? हमारा समाधान है बहुभाषी कन्टेन्ट रणनीति।

हिंदी कन्टेन्ट की खपत 94% की दर से बढ़ रही है।

अंग्रेजी, ज़ाहिर है, न केवल दुनिया में बल्कि भारत में भी सबसे अधिक इस्तेमाल की जाने वाली भाषा है। हालांकि, गूगल डेटा हिंदी कन्टेन्ट उपभोग में 94% की वृद्धि दर दिखाता है। इसे ध्यान में रखते हुए वैश्विक ब्रांडों ने अपनी रणनीति की कला के रूप में क्षेत्रीय भाषा पर ध्यान केंद्रित करना शुरू कर दिया है। एक साल पहले, फेसबुक यूज़र्स लॉग इन पेज हिंदी स्क्रिप्ट में देख कर हैरान हो गए थे। इसके बाद अमेरिका आधारित दृश्य खोज टूल पिनट्रस्ट ने एक हिंदी संस्करण लॉन्च किया, जिससे भारत के उपयोगकर्ताओं को अनुवादित संस्करण का उपयोग करने की सुविधा मिल गई। आज, गूगल अन्य भाषाओं के साथ हिंदी, गुजराती, मराठी, बंगाली और तमिल जैसी भाषाओं को भी सपोर्ट करता है। भारत में 234 मिलियन इंटरनेट उपयोगकर्ता स्थानीय भाषा के कन्टेन्ट का उपभोग करते हैं, सभी वैश्विक सोशल मीडिया साइटों ने इस तथ्य को महसूस किया है कि अगर वे भारत में स्थानीय नहीं जाते हैं तो वे जल्द प्रासंगिकता खो सकते हैं। द्वितीय और तृतीय टियर के शहरों के इंटरनेट उपयोगकर्ताओं की

आवश्यकताओं को पूरा करते हुए, गूगल अब अपने उत्पादों जैसे गूगल मैप के उपयोग को स्थानीय भाषाओं में, खासकर हिंदी में, विस्तारित करने पर ध्यान केंद्रित कर रहा है।

क्षेत्रीय कन्टेन्ट की उपलब्धता भारत में इंटरनेट की वृद्धि को 24% तक बढ़ा सकती है।

74% साक्षरों में से, केवल 10% लोग अंग्रेजी पढ़ते हैं, जबकि बाकी लोग स्थानीय भाषा में कन्टेन्ट का उपभोग करते हैं। शेष 66% अपनी स्थानीय भाषा में साक्षर हैं। इंटरनेट और मोबाइल एसोसिएशन ऑफ इंडिया और IMRB इंटरनेशनल द्वारा किए गए एक नवीनतम अध्ययन के अनुसार, क्षेत्रीय कन्टेन्ट की उपलब्धता भारत में इंटरनेट के विकास को 24% तक बढ़ावा दे सकती है। भारत में 70,000 से ज्यादा अख़बार छपते हैं और लगभग 90% या तो हिंदी में या अन्य प्रादेशिक भाषाओं में छपते हैं। क्षेत्रीय कन्टेन्ट के महत्व को महसूस करते हुए, भारतीय ऐप डेवलपर स्थानीय ऐप वितरण प्लेटफ़ॉर्म की आवश्यकता को भी पहचान रहे हैं। अंतर्राष्ट्रीय ऐप स्टोर खुद को अत्यधिक भारत-विशिष्ट क्षेत्रीय कन्टेन्ट की आसान खोज में अनुकूलित नहीं करते हैं।

क्षेत्रीय भाषा के कन्टेन्ट का विकास: एक मामले का अध्ययन

उद्यमियों और उद्यमशील पारिस्थितिकी तंत्र को बढ़ावा देने के लिए भारत के प्रमुख मंचों में से एक, Yourstory.com ने, हाल ही में क्षेत्रीय कन्टेन्ट के लिए अलग-अलग अनुभाग शामिल किया है।

उनकी क्षेत्रीय सामग्री रणनीति बहुत अच्छी तरह से बनाई गई है और दर्शकों से उसे सकारात्मक प्रतिक्रिया प्राप्त हुई है।

जैसा कि आप देख सकते हैं, हिंदी के लेखों के 650 शेयर हुए हैं और तमिल कन्टेन्ट के 200 से अधिक शेयर हुए हैं। वेबसाइट अपने क्षेत्रीय भाषा के पेजों को दिलचस्प लेखों के साथ हर रोज अपडेट कर रही है। वेबसाइट 10 अन्य भाषाओं में भी सामग्री प्रदान करती है जिसमें मराठी, तेलगू और बंगाली शामिल हैं।

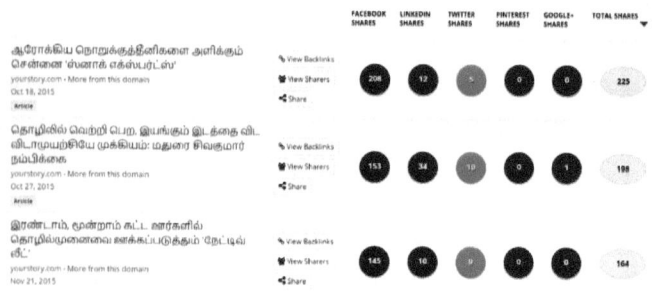

इसलिए यदि आपको विश्वास है कि क्षेत्रीय कन्टेन्ट विपणन महत्वपूर्ण है, तो यहां पर विचार करने के लिए कुछ चीजें दी गई हैं।

1. दर्शक प्राप्त होना और ग्लोबल SEO संचालित करना

यदि एक प्रमुख भाषा बहुमत बनाती है, तो अन्य भाषाओं को अनदेखा करना आसान होता है। हालांकि अंग्रेजी बहुमत बनाती है, एक ऐसा भी खंड है जो केवल एक क्षेत्रीय भाषा में ही कन्टेन्ट का उपयोग करता है और यह खंड आपके सबसे महत्वपूर्ण लक्षित दर्शकों के रूप में हो सकता है। एक अंग्रेजी रचना 0.1% से 0.15% क्लिक थू अनुपात (CTR) प्राप्त करती है, जबकि एक भाषाई रचना 0.4–0.5% CTR प्राप्त कर सकती है। इसलिए अगर एक भाषा की सामग्री और रचना में आपके उत्पाद या वेबसाइट पर अधिक ट्रैफ़िक आकर्षित करने की संभावना है, तो उस पर अधिक ध्यान क्यों न दें?

2. ग्राहक अपनी मातृभाषा के कन्टेन्ट पर बेहतर प्रतिक्रिया करते हैं

जब आप अपने ब्रांड की एक क्षेत्रीय भाषा में मार्केटिंग करते हैं, तो यह दर्शकों के भावनात्मक भाग को आकर्षित करता है। इसलिए कन्टेन्ट का स्थानीयकरण (लोकलाईजेशन) सृजन प्रक्रिया का अभिन्न अंग होना चाहिए। उदाहरण के लिए, मैकडॉनल्ड्स उत्पाद विकास के शुरुआती चरण में अपनी अंतरराष्ट्रीय

टीमों को शामिल करता है, यह सुनिश्चित करता है कि जहां उसके अभियान चल रहे हैं, वहां के प्रत्येक विशिष्ट संस्कृति के लिए अपनी सबसे अधिक प्रभावी मार्केटिंग रणनीतियों का अनुकूलन कर सकता है। इसकी स्थानीय अनुवाद और स्थानीयकरण (लोकलाईजेशन) टीम सुनिश्चित करती है कि कन्टेन्ट प्रत्येक देश में उपयुक्त तरीके से लिखे जाते हैं।

3. सोशल मीडिया और कन्टेन्ट मार्केटिंग को एकीकृत करना

सोशल मीडिया में भाग लेने का आपका अंतिम लक्ष्य अपनी वेबसाइट पर ट्रैफिक वापस ले जाने की संभावना है ताकि आप उन दर्शकों को लीड में परिवर्तित कर सकें। एक बार जब आपकी क्षेत्रीय कन्टेन्ट तैयार हो जाता है और चलने लगता है, तब उस रणनीति को अपने सोशल मीडिया और पेड विज्ञापन के साथ एकीकृत करना एक बढ़िया विचार होगा। यह उपभोक्ताओं को आकर्षित करने के लिए महत्वपूर्ण हो सकता है और कई ब्रांड अपने विदेशी मार्केटिंग प्रयासों में इसे सफलतापूर्वक अपना रहे हैं।

Marketing Mix Insights

Marketing for Companies: Time to Shift from Print to Digital Media?

In this age of new media marketing, digital marketing has proved to be a game-changer. While any proponent of an effective marketing mix model would suggest a healthy mix of conventional as well as unconventional modes, digital media certainly leads by a margin, when you bring the ROI perspective into play. The advent of digital media has paved way for a marketing approach that now wants to track penny-to-penny spent on each marketing effort and the returns derived from it.

Digital marketing is predominantly being used by every firm out there and is proving to be an extremely successful means of spreading awareness and creating a brand value. The same is true for all industries.

The challenge is stiff competition in the market

The biggest challenge for the big companies is that in this highly competitive space, the brands are looking forward to boosting their digital presence and generating leads. In order to enable these companies to establish a digital identity and leverage upon it, they need foolproof innovative digital marketing strategies with lead generation at the center stage.

Website should be user-friendly and mobile responsive

There are a couple of things to be kept in mind while designing a website and implementing digital marketing strategies for real estate companies. First and foremost, it is the website that needs attention. The purpose of the website could vary from capturing leads to brand building. A website must be user-friendly and must ensure "call-to-action." Great content always helps in increasing visibility on the digital media.

Creative usage of social media to build brand and generate leads

On social media platforms like Facebook, Twitter, Pinterest, Google Plus, what matters is how creative your content is. The frequency is not an issue as long as your posts are able to garner enough audience engagement. Real estate companies need to project their unique strengths in the most creative manner possible on the digital space. A lot of online tools and applications are available nowadays that help in automated updates on the social media sites.

SEO to rank higher in search results

Social media follows SEO. Earlier, the pre-conceived notion was that just having a website is enough. But actually, just having a website takes us nowhere. Search Engine Optimization and Search Engine Marketing play a key role in the integrated approach towards getting traffic on the website and generating leads. SEO results give an imperative method of ranking on the digital space and the higher the company is ranked, the better its chances of gaining leads from their websites.

Print media v/s Digital media: Digital gives a better ROI

Let's take an example from the real estate industry.

Traditionally, real estate companies invest highly in print ads, but the returns they get on their investments is comparatively lower when compared to the Google ads. Our research in the space threw up a couple of interesting facts. The research results clearly show that on investing the same amount of money in digital marketing and print media, real estate companies are able to realize results which are approximately 2.5 times better. The detailed statistics are as shown below in the table:

	PRINT ADS	GOOGLE ADS	ASSUMPTIONS
Advertising Spend	Rs. 7,00,000	Rs. 7,00,000	The print ad costs have been considered based on the cost of 1/4th page advertisement in a national daily
Visitors to the website	420	10000	Assuming Rs. 70 per click for targeted Google ads & 0.06% reach to the target segment in case of print ads
No. of leads	130	400	Assumed 30 web leads & 100 call leads for print ads and a traffic to lead conversion rate of 4% for Google ads
No. of site visits	32.5	100	Assumed 25% conversion of leads into site visits
Buyers (Final Conversions)	3.25	10	Considered 10% of site visits to final conversion

*ROI comparison for Print v/s Digital media

A quarter page advertisement in a newspaper cost about Rs. 7 lakhs, which is bound to target one million or more people. However, the conversion rate is surprisingly low. One print ad worth Rs. 7 lakhs results in about 400 website visits, out of which about 130 leads are generated. In the end, the company gets only three to four buyers for the properties on an average. In comparison, Google ads, with the similar investment of Rs. 7 lakhs, result in about 400 leads, which convert into more than ten buyers.

The way forward for all industries: it is never too late

Most of the companies currently do not have a commendable social media presence, but it's never too late. There is immense potential in the digital media to leverage for the companies. The efficiency and optimization control should be at the forefront of any decision by an organization. And when that decision has the potential to catapult the number of leads by 250%, then there is no reason why real estate companies should not go digital.

Sector Specific Solutions

The Ultimate Guide to Digital Marketing for the Financial Industry

Digital marketing is the go-to form of marketing, whether you are a small-scale start up or a well-established global brand. The power of the Internet has engulfed our day-to-day lives and all types of industries – from Retail and Travel to Real Estate and B2B – have joined the digital wave. However, digital marketing for the financial industry has taken a backseat in the branding bandwagon. Though many reputed banks and financial organizations are setting foot into the digital revolution by allotting a bulk of their marketing budgets to online branding, they are yet to completely go digital. Let's take a look at the various ways, in which digital marketing for the finance industry can prove to be a big boon to the sector.

Benefits of Digital Marketing for the Financial Industry

To widen their clientele

With over 450 million active users on the Internet, India is the world's second biggest online community. The figures are estimated to increase to a whopping 635 million by the end of 2021. These stunning statistics are proof that digital marketing for the financial industry is a guaranteed way to reach a large percentage of the Indian population and convert them to loyal customers.

To evaluate their services

The dynamic medium of the Internet is a two-way street. Apart from providing financial sectors with an excellent platform to market their brand and feature their products, the online space also offers the benefit of evaluating your services and seeing what works. You will also have complete access to analytics and other such statistical data to track the performance of your digital campaigns.

To receive instant feedback

Customer satisfaction is of vital importance in the finance sector. Ensuring your consumers are happy and satisfied with your services is what drives the banking sector, and digital marketing for the finance industry offers just that. From online posts to discussion forums, you will get a closer insight into what your customers are looking for in your products and how you can improvise your services for better consumer delight.

To cut down on marketing costs

There is no doubt that marketing your brand on the digital space costs much lesser that traditional advertising and branding. Apart from comparatively lesser costing, financial organizations will also get a better reach and can target their audience more effectively. Banks and other financial institutes can take complete advantage of this cost efficiency and resorting to digital marketing for the financial industry as their branding strategy.

Top Ways of Using Digital Marketing for the Finance Industry

With such intense benefits, it is time all leading banks and institutes in the financial sector hop onto the digital bandwagon and sail strong along the digital wave. Here are few of the ways in which you can kick-start your online journey.

Digitize your brand

Banks and other organizations in the financial sector can leverage digital marketing for the financial sector as their branding strategy by working neck-and-neck with a digital agency. These agencies, such as Social Beat, provide end-to-end digital solutions from social media posts that go viral to top-notch website content that will rank you in the first page of Google.

Create an engaging app

There are an estimated 300 million smartphone users in India and this statistic is expected to reach a mind-boggling 2.3 billion by the end of 2022. With such a large percentage of the Indian population relying on apps for their daily chores, it is time you dive into the digital space with a high-end app, designed to cater to every need of your customers.

Whether you are a leading bank or a financial data aggregator, investing in a good app is a guaranteed way to take your business to towering heights. In today's day and age, people like to be on the move even while making financial plans or surfing the internet for research. Apart from merely searching for information, most money transfers and other financial transactions also happen over the phone. With a user-friendly app, all your services and programs will be available at the click of a button, which will lead to higher lead conversions and ultimately, customer satisfaction.

You can also explore the concept of Progressive Web Apps for your company. This phenomenon is one of the top digital marketing trends in 2018 and is guaranteed to change the outlook of your financial organization.

Go social

Financial institutes can increase the exposure of the organization by tapping on the reach of social media marketing. India is leading the online community with 241 million active users on Facebook. This only means that a large number of potential customers are currently scrolling through their social feeds and there is a possibility that a lump sum of this audience is in the lookout of a reliable and reputed financial partner. With relatable social media posts, financial organizations can easily use content to engage with their target audience and widen their consumer database. You can also track the performance of your posts through advanced social media analytics Tools and strategize accordingly.

FundsIndia is India's biggest online investment platform with over 1 million consumers. In one of their most recent Facebook campaigns, on investing in mutual funds, they targeted the women of India with a quirky creative and copy.

Get ranked

In today's day and age, the first thing that pops in a consumer's mind while looking for a particular service or product is to perform a mobile search. If you are considering digital marketing for the finance industry, one of your first steps should be to ensure you rank on Google. Focusing on optimal Search Engine Optimization will drive a higher traffic to your website, which, in turn, will lead to higher lead conversions.

You can start by ensuring your organization is featured on Google local listings to increase the footfall to your outlets. You can also get showcased on Google My Business listings to give potential customers a brief insight of your organization. Apart from Google listings it is also a good idea to leverage the power of content marketing to get ranked. You can promote your services and packages with engaging blogs and other posts that have the potential to both rank on Google and go viral on social media. However, make sure you explore all content amplification strategies to promote your content. It is also vital to incorporate all the keywords and trending topics in your blog posts for better results.

Step up your ad game

Facebook and Google ads have taken the world of digital advertising by storm. From website conversion ads to carousel and lead ads, banks can opt for an array of advertising techniques to drive enquiries and quality leads. You can also market your brand with a creative combination of videos, images and copy to attract your target group. Facebook is the best bet when it comes to online advertising as you can opt for detailed targeting based on age, geographic location, content consumption, online behavior and many other such demographics. You can also target the users who have previously clicked on your ad or recently visited your website for leads of premium quality.

A Google ad is the other "non-social" type of ad financial organizations and can invest in to widen their clientele. These ads show up in Google, when potential customers type in the relevant keywords in search of a renowned banking institute.

Engage your audience with drip marketing

Email marketing is the most traditional and effective type of online branding, especially when it comes to digital marketing for the financial industry. With the beginning of 2018, this trend has been upgraded with an improvised version of customized emails. Reaching out to your potential consumers with personalized emails featuring the various offers and packages provided by your organization is a guaranteed way of increasing lead conversions. For example, if a user has logged into your website and shown interest in your services by subscribing to your newsletter, you can nurture the lead with regular notifications and offers provided by your firm to attract them further. According to a recent survey, drip email marketing provides a 119% click-through rate on authentic emails.

Apart from lead nurturing, drip emailers are also effective triggers to close incomplete transactions. For example, if a user had clicked on one of your financial programs or was in the middle of a transaction, but could not complete the task, your digital team can target them with follow-up emails as gentle reminders. The emails can be customized as per the demographics of the user, with an effective call-to-action to close the deal in a single click. Featured below is one of the creative used in a drip emailer for one of our top clients – Kotak Asset Management who has engaged with digital marketing for the finance industry.

Use word-of-mouth marketing

Influencer marketing is one of the top digital marketing trends of 2017 and is expected to continue its reign in 2018. There is a personal element of trust and assurance, when customers choose their financial partners based on the advice and suggestions of a commoner and that is exactly the type of branding influencer marketing has to offer. Influencers upload engaging posts and modest reviews in the form of blogs, videos and pictures, which has the potential to instantly attract viewers and convert them to consumers. Influencer marketing is one of the main pillars of digital marketing for the finance industry and is definitely something you should leverage for your organization.

Financial Organizations and Digital Marketing – A Case Study

The potential of going social – Bank of Baroda

Bank of Baroda is one of the first public banking organizations to have resorted to digital marketing for the financial industry. Their marketing team focused on creating a premium presence on the online space rather than giving plain emphasis on the number of followers. Each of their campaigns had a specific objective from promotional content to lead generation. One of their most commendable campaigns was that of "One in a leap." In this campaign, the bank put up a post on Facebook asking their customers to tag the one person who is a role model in their lives. The post was put up on 29 February during the leap year of 2016. The hashtag #OneInALeap was trending for a good six hours along with the hot topic of the day – the Indian Union Budget 2016.

Powerful story telling – ICICI Bank

Being one of the leading banks in the nation, ICICI tapped the Indian female population with the #FundYourOwnGrowth campaign. The campaign focused on encouraging women to invest in themselves and not be tied down by the shackles of the society. Women around the subcontinent could enroll in the Fund Your Own Growth program and open a woman's account to enjoy a plethora of irresistible offers and benefits. A lot of online traffic was driven to their website, which showcased the program details, advantages of opening a woman's account and a series of inspirational stories of real women and their struggles against poverty. Through this campaign, the bank took the angle of empowering women to sell a financial product. The campaign also included a 2-Minute Video Ad featuring top Indian actor Konkana Sen Sharma, which was splashed on all major digital video platforms, including YouTube.

The magic of Google ads – BijliPay

Apart from banks and leading monetary institutes, B2B organizations that cater to the technologies involved in the financial sector are also focusing on digital marketing for the financial industry. BijliPay, one of India's top end-to-end providers of payment solutions, collaborated with Social Beat to up their digital game and gain quality leads from the online space.

When the Rs 1000 and Rs 500 notes were demonetized in the end of 2016, a lot of businesses realized the need to go digital in order to survive in the market. Understanding this demand, BijliPay used Google to advertise their mPOS devices (card swiping machines). The primary objective of the campaigns was to acquire more customers in the wake of Demonetisation. In order to achieve our targets, we performed AB testing for different landing pages and altered the copies of various search campaigns based on what was performing well. Our groundbreaking campaigns landed 3,569 lead conversions with a cost per conversion of just Rs 285.

With such astounding statistics and mind-boggling figures, there is no doubt that digital marketing for the finance industry is an emerging trend which is here to stay. It is time you leverage the power of digital and secure the future of your financial organization.

How Digital Marketing Will Transform Real Estate Industry in 2018

Over the last few years, digital marketing has played a key role in the advertising and branding of an organization. Apart from uplifting the brand image, going digital also helps in reaching the target audience which, in turn, aids in generating leads and promoting sales.

One such industry that has tried, tested and achieved significant business growth with digital marketing is Real Estate and there is more to come in 2018. The last decade has witnessed a lot of real estate activity in the online space. A lot of property buyers and sellers do vigorous research online, before they ultimately make the purchase or sell the property offline. Hence, making sure you have a strong online presence is of utmost importance to make your brand name stand out in the real estate industry.

So, what makes digital marketing for real estate such a vital tool for developers and home seekers alike and how is it going to progress going forward? To find out, let's take a flashback to how it all began. Digital Media Facts & Stats:

- 462 million Internet users
- 200 million active social media users (over 60% college are college students)

- The digital marketplace has grown by 33% between 2010 and 2015
- 77% of online users buy products exclusively on social media
- 50% of shoppers buy online based on social media influence
- 74% of buyers rely on influence for making purchase decisions
- The sale of physical goods through the digital space amounted to 16.8 billion dollars in revenue

Digital Marketing for Real Estate Stats (July 2016)

- 14% of home buyers search for tips on how to purchase homes more effectively
- 42% of home buyers have used the Internet as their first search medium
- 82% of home buyers trust online agents as good information sources
- 92% home buyers have searched for homes the Internet

The Benefits of Real Estate Digital Marketing

Marketing techniques are open to evolve and get better over time. Additionally, if you are an ardent user of the digital space for marketing your products, you know it comes with numerous benefits. Apart from the urban space, digital marketing is evolving in tier II and tier III cities of India as well. Real estate developers are yet to realize these benefits and are only scratching the surface when it comes to taking full advantage of what digital marketing has to offer. Here's where digital marketing in real estate gives developers an edge, with a multitude of digital marketing trends.

- **Cost-efficient:** Needless to say, there is a lot of money that goes into a real estate project. Digital marketing offers free publicity at comparatively lower pricing to that of traditional marketing, so it's no surprise that marketers in the real estate industry are taking full advantage of the cost efficiency.

- **Increased exposure:** Considering the numerous housing projects that vary in size, location and cost, having a digital marketing strategy lets you expand your overall reach and even customize that reach towards a selected target market.

- **Performance Analysis:** Digital marketing offers numerous ways to keep track of an advertisement's performance in the competitive marketplace, making it easier for real estate developers to understand what marketing technique works best for their products.

- **Creative license:** Be it an apartment, independent house, villa or a plot of land, there are numerous ways for developers to showcase their products in the online marketplace.

- **Brand building:** To succeed in the vast industry that is Real Estate, developers need a strong and reputable presence. Having online presence is considered the next best brand building technique.

Marketing Techniques That Work Wonders

For any company, which is hoping to succeed in the digital space, there are three goals every digital marketer must try and achieve:

1. Building the brand
2. Acquiring customers
3. Customer engagement

Let us look at some digital marketing practices (in the Real Estate Industry) that will help achieve the above-mentioned goals.

1. Building the Brand

Creating an online presence is the first, most important step, and serves as a backbone for all future digital marketing activities. To establish a powerful online presence, real estate developers need to focus on creating three things.

Creating a Website

For real estate, a website can serve two purposes: a virtual office that showcases the builder's latest projects or a virtual marketplace for home seekers to explore purchasing options. To make either one or both of these purposes work well, there are numerous tools and optimization techniques that need to be implemented.

Even the design of the website matters as it can make a difference to user experience and one such design that has been making waves amongst the real estate websites is a flat design. Flat website designs are categorized by their simple, elegant and square'ish' look; first noticed in the Windows 8 Tile User Interface. With minimalistic animations and loads of white space, the flat website design has proven to be effective in page speed loading times, readability, mobile optimization and ease of navigation.

While a good website design is pleasing to the eyes, it only scratches the surface of what matters especially in the Real Estate sector. A stellar design needs to be accompanied with great content to create an impact. Writing good content that effectively communicates a real estate brand's message and intrigues the user to go ahead for a purchase is vital. Presenting your target audience with engaging content is a sure-shot way to grab their attention and generate leads.

Real Estate is a very broad topic, so to fit everything into a single website, other strategies can be utilized to showcase everything a Real Estate developer has to offer.

- **Multiple Web pages:** Aside from having a homepage that gives a gist of the Real Estate builder's brand, having multiple web pages that provide more information on the brand and interlink with one another through clever content navigation is essential. More pages ultimately result in users spending more time on the website, which directly affects the website's rank on search engines.
- **Landing Pages:** Landing pages act as mini e-commerce portals that explain in detail about a particular brand's upcoming, on-going or released Real Estate project. Landing pages that are interactive or those that have video presentations have proven to yield 403% more inquiries than regular pages.

Search Engine Optimization (SEO)

- SEO is the glue that holds an entire digital marketing campaign together. As a matter of fact, digital marketers for Real Estate must have an SEO Planner right at the beginning of their marketing strategy. From SEO Plugins to various Link Building Techniques, the driving force of good SEO, especially for Real Estate, is keyword research.
- Statistics show that 80% of home buyers search for properties online, which means having a list of search keywords incorporated into a content marketing strategy will pay off well. Potential customers will most likely be presented with search results about a property that has those keywords. Additionally, real estate companies can also leverage local SEO and Google Maps to promote their business.

Creating a Blog

When people need help or are looking for something, they do one of two things – seek out a person or a place or browse the internet. Blogging has come a long way from being a casual online tool for storytelling to an essential element of a digital marketing strategy.

Blogs are a long, short or creative source of information and if there is one thing Google loves, it is loads of valuable information. Research shows that websites with blogs have 434% more indexed pages. Google recognizes and ranks these websites easily due to the information provided, ultimately leading to that site showing up on the first page of search results.

Considering how broad a topic Real Estate is, builders must take advantage of the power of blogging and focus on sharing information to potential home buyers. Blogs that give detailed information on upcoming properties, tips on home buying and guides on investment options are just some of the many topics a real estate blog can include.

Having a strong social media presence

The platform of social media offers brands a unique way to get more personal with their audience, and it is no different in the case of real estate.

There are numerous platforms for social media marketing available today and some of the most useful ones for Real Estate developers include:

- **Facebook:** India has the world's largest number of Facebook users (195 million and counting), so there is a clear and open platform for Real Estate developers to take advantage of the numerous advertising techniques Facebook has to offer.

- **YouTube:** Videos are without a doubt, the most watched medium on the planet. Real estate developers can use Optimized YouTube videos to add a layer of instructiveness to their promotional campaigns.
- **Twitter:** This micro-blogging giant has proven to be a rather useful marketing tool in the recent years. Twitter serves as a great platform for real estate developers to invite credible 3rd party sources to influence purchase decisions. For more insight on this, make sure you check out our extensive Twitter marketing guide for businesses in India.
- **LinkedIn:** LinkedIn is the go-to medium for anyone looking to expand their business to business portfolio. Real estate developers can connect to third party realtors, architects, interior designers, house maintenance providers and so on.

2. Acquiring Customers

Having an online presence will not be fruitful if your potential customers are not aware of that presence. Real Estate developers depend heavily on lead generation, and digital marketing offers the quickest, easiest and most ROI friendly lead generation method. Here are some of the ways real estate developers can acquire customers via digital media.

Advertising

Advertising online is one of the best ways to ensure you are reaching your potential target group. If done right, it can be the best lead generation tool for real estate developers. Be it Facebook, Google or even other platforms such as Bing and Yahoo, using lead generation, website conversion ads or even interactive ads to engage with your target audience and collect leads.

Facebook Ads

As of July 2017, there are 241 million active users in India on Facebook. This is a primary reason why advertising on Facebook is something every builder needs to try. From website conversion ads to lead ads and carousel ads, builders should try a combination of videos and images to drive enquiries and site visits. Facebook also has detailed targeting by demographics, age and behavior. Additionally, you can also target your website visitors and those you have engaged with your post so that the ad is displayed to a more specific and niche crowd making the probability of selling the property even higher than before.

Ads in regional languages have started rolling out, and marketers have begun incorporating this concept into their marketing strategies to reach out to their target audience. When a potential home buyer reads an ad in his regional language, he develops a bond of trust and comfort with the seller and is more likely to make a purchase or at least recommend that product to a friend.

With Facebook's brand reach and frequency campaigns, brands can even get assured visibility and reach, similar to what a front-page newspaper ad gives.

Google Ads

Google AdWords is a paid digital marketing strategy that is run on the Google search engine. Adwords Smart Display Campaigns run strongly through a set of rules and guidelines and work best when incorporated into SEO tools and strategies.

Let us say a home seeker is typing "flats in OMR" in the search box. If the digital marketer has incorporated the keywords "flats in OMR" along with some other relevant search queries, Google will pick up that ad and display it in the search results.

The placement of the ad depends entirely on the budget set for the campaign. You can also optimize your adwords campaign for profound results.

Drip email marketing

Drip emails are automated emails that are sent out based on a predefined time or user actions. Real Estate developers can target and constantly stay in touch with a group of people based on certain criteria retrieved from a strong email-marketing database. Let us say that a customer has visited a property website and shown interest by subscribing to property newsletters. Digital marketers can use the information provided by the customer to send emails about the development and completion of the property and news on various other related properties.

Drip emails are a powerful lead nurturer, with statistics showing a 119% increase click-through rate via trustworthy emails.

Influencer marketing

Influencer marketing is the Internet's word-of-mouth marketing method and can prove very effective to generate leads for real estate developers. Just like word-of-mouth, influencer marketing uses popular bloggers and other professionals in the real estate industry to promote a particular property. Influencer marketing channels include both blogs and social media channels, so Real estate developers must carefully choose the appropriate kind of influencer to market their properties.

Influencer. in provides a one-stop platform for real estate developers to search and connect with the best influencers in the country; they can choose from either working on long campaigns with a selected influencer or contacting multiple micro-influencers over various social media platforms to spread the word.

3. Customer Engagement

The age-old marketing rule of getting new customers while retaining existing customers applies in the digital space as well. Of course, the most popular tool for customer engagement today is social media, and Facebook ranks high up on the list, especially for the real estate industry. There is a plethora of social media trends benefiting the real estate industry. Here are some interesting ways developers can utilize Facebook and YouTube for customer engagement.

Facebook engagement

- Post real estate investment advice albeit with a funny picture
- Post product comparison images and let the followers vote
- Post interesting facts about the locality where the property is being developed
- Post about celebrity or high-profile activity that is happening in the locality where the property is being developed
- Post about festivals and celebratory occasions while adding a twist that relates to a property
- Share information about daily real estate activities

YouTube engagement

- Post videos on property interiors
- DIY practical tips on home improvement
- Property reviews
- Live feed of upcoming events that relate to the property
- Virtual reality property experience

Case Study: Digital Marketing for a Leading Real Estate Developer in Chennai

One of our esteemed clients is a Chennai based Real Estate enterprise, which laid its foundations in 2004. Known for providing niche residential segments like luxury villas and high-rise apartments, the company has since produced 68 projects, selling to over 4000 happy residents.

Our client wanted to scale up its digital presence through powerful digital marketing, focusing on five primary goals.

- Improved UX Design
- SEO
- SMM
- Influencer Marketing
- Digital Advertising

An intense digital marketing campaign followed, running on platforms like Facebook, LinkedIn and Google search, resulting in an impressive turnaround that showed:

- Over 500 crore in sales from digital enquiries
- 10x increase in lead generation
- Cost per lead reduction by 30%
- Organic traffic increase by 3x
- 4x increase in leads from organic traffic
- Fan base on Facebook has grown to an engaged community of over 1,40,000 fans

Real estate is the most reliable and secure long-term investment you can make, and the ability to purchase a home will only get easier with newer technologies coming into the digital space. These technologies are capable of giving you a real-time experience of any property through a screen.

How Digital Marketing for FMCG Brands Will Revolutionize the Sector

Digital media is changing the landscape for marketers everywhere, especially in the FMCG sector. Traditionally, campaigns for every FMCG product would depend on determining the right marketing mix of the 4P's (Product, Price, Place and Promotion) that would best influence the target audience's purchase decisions. Today, however, consumers are making buying-decisions differently and with this, strategies aimed at impacting this process need to evolve as well.

Consumers are exposed to their phone and laptop screens more than they are to traditional media like television, newspapers and billboards. There is also a growing number of consumers who prefer to shop online for FMCG products rather than visit a physical store. According to a report by Google and Bain and Co., $11 billion or two-thirds, of the total sales in beauty and hygiene products will be influenced through online marketing. In today's digital era, a strong digital marketing strategy is indispensable for FMCG brands.

Adapting the 4P's for Digital Marketing

Digital marketing for FMCG companies doesn't mean retiring the tried and tested 4P's, which formed the holy grail of marketing for years. Instead, it involves tweaking the marketing mix for

FMCG products to bring them into the current era. Digital marketing trends in FMCG allow marketers to not just capture the consumer at the final buying stage, but also to establish a relationship with them from the start, something that was not possible before. This requires marketers to formulate a holistic FMCG digital strategy to not just influence their consumers, but to also personally engage with them.

How Digital Marketing Can Benefit FMCG Brands

Incorporating a strong digital marketing strategy in the overall marketing mix offers many clear advantages to brands.

1. It Helps Distinguish Your Brand

The FMCG sector is marked by a large variety of similar products, which offer consumers a wide range to choose from. One of the biggest advantages of having an effective digital marketing strategy in place is that it helps brands create a unique brand identity. This helps consumers form a strong opinion of the brand, which will ultimately influence their purchase decision.

2. It Provides an Innovative Way to Display Your Brand

In traditional marketing for FMCG, the product display was considered one of the most important factors, which influenced purchase decisions. Consumers are visual creatures, so the more attractive your packaging, the higher the chance of it being noticed by them. In the same way, digital marketing for FMCG companies can be approached as a virtual shelf display. It is even more effective than a physical display because it helps you reach your specific target audience, making your overall marketing strategy more cost-effective. This enables top-of-mind awareness, which can influence purchase decisions. Like physical shelves, digital marketing also allows you to position your products contextually. Through tools like AdWords Smart Display, you can showcase your products while consumers browse through similar categories. For example, if you are a skincare brand, you can display your ads next to beauty blogs your consumers are browsing through.

3. It Allows You to Gain Consumer Insights and Increase ROI

One of the biggest advantages digital marketing has over traditional marketing is that it helps you track every facet of your marketing efforts. FMCG brands spend large sums on hoardings, TV commercials, print ads, radio ads and more. However, the results of these campaigns are very difficult to measure effectively. While speculative figures can be produced, there is no way to arrive at a definite conclusion.

Digital marketing, on the other hand, helps you track and measure every aspect of your campaign. With the help of analytic tools, brands can recover information about number of impressions, clicks, conversions and more. It also lets them find out exactly which ad prompted the consumer to make the purchase. Advanced analytics can even let you gain deep consumer insights. This can help you create campaigns and content that your target audience will actually find engaging. With the ease of tracking digital marketing offers, FMCG brands can refine their strategies and make it more cost-effective.

4. Mobile Usage Is Only Going to Grow from Here

Offline purchases might still form the bulk of FMCG sales, but the future belongs to mobile phones. Mobile phones and high-speed, affordable internet have penetrated almost every section of the Indian audience. A significant portion of Indian consumers is shopping for FMCG products online through various apps and this number is only going to grow. Digital marketing trends in

FMCG need to keep up with the increasing volume of customers who prefer to shop online.

One of the biggest areas of growth in mobile usage will be in tier 2 cities and small towns in India. FMCG brands need to stay up-to-date on the constantly evolving digital marketing trends in these tier II and tier III cities. Unless brands solidify their FMCG digital strategy now, they are going to witness severe drawbacks in the future.

FMCG Digital Strategy Techniques

Digital media offers a number of streams for FMCG brands to market themselves. These various platforms also help brands meet a number of marketing objectives, right from creating awareness and brand building to driving conversions and cultivating brand loyalty.

1. Build Strong Communities Through Content Marketing

For a long time, the focus of marketing strategies for FMCG brands revolved around a one-way promotion of their products. Today, however, digital marketing trends in FMCG are shifting the focus to creating user-centric content that brings actual value to consumers' lives. By creating informative content, you can drive conversations among your consumers and build strong communities. Having a solid community is crucial to developing a loyal consumer base. Digital marketing can help strengthen your brand's community through a number of innovative content marketing strategies that work.

Clever use of content marketing is essential because it helps establish your authority in the space. For example, Johnson & Johnson created BabyCenter.com, a website for moms to share information and engage through helpful forums. While not overtly a part of Johnson & Johnson, all ads displayed on BabyCenter.

com were for the brand. This allowed Johnson & Johnson to build a strong community of moms that they could tap into to sell their products. This kind of user-focused marketing is unique to digital marketing and helps brands promote their products more effectively than ever before.

Another facet of content marketing that is essential for FMCG brands is creating SEO-friendly content. Incorporating a strong SEO plan as well as including strategies for content amplification is crucial because it drives consumers to your website, enabling them to become more aware of your brand. Keyword-optimized content also helps consumers find you when they have a query, which goes a long way in establishing your brand's credibility in that domain.

2. Strengthen Digital Presence Through Social Media

Facebook is undeniably one of the biggest avenues for digital marketing. Through advanced tools for social media analytics, you can find your target audience, refine your marketing strategy and even drive conversions. The Facebook custom audience tool can help you widen your target audience and reach them through your campaigns. FMCG brands can also use Facebook to get deeper insights into consumer behavior.

However, your consumers are not using only Facebook and as a brand, neither should you. Digital marketing for FMCG brands needs to be integrated over various channels to have the maximum impact. This includes ads, which play before a YouTube video, promotions through Twitter, Instagram posts and much more. Effective digital marketing for FMCG even includes SEO-friendly content, so your brand shows up when consumers search for a related need. With an increase in the number of FMCG products showing up online, Google Ads are also another important avenue for FMCG marketing.

3. Consistently Engage With Your Audience to Encourage Brand Loyalty

Traditionally, FMCG advertisements were a one-way interaction, with brands informing consumers about their products over TV commercials, radio spots and print ads. Advertising was done mostly when there was a new product or service to promote. Buying space in traditional media is expensive and only allows for a one-way communication. This is why brands were unable to consistently engage with their consumers.

Digital media is changing all of that permanently. Digital marketing has a clear edge over traditional marketing when it comes to generating user engagement. Digital marketing trends in FMCG products are aimed towards establishing your brand as a constant presence in your consumers' lives. Through shareable content, helpful information and meaningful interaction, brands can continue to stay relevant at all times. This helps consumers recall your brand at the time of making a purchase decision. Whole Foods, for example, utilized chatbots in their digital marketing strategy to engage consumers and direct them towards completing a purchase.

4. Widen Consumer Base Through Influencer Marketing

Influencer marketing is proving to be one of the most important digital marketing trends in FMCG. With influencers, your brand can tap into their huge number of followers and increase consumer awareness of your products. Influencer marketing is also very useful for FMCG brands because consumers are more likely to believe in the credibility of your brand when an influencer whom they trust recommends it to them.

5. Drip Email Marketing

A one-size-fits-all marketing campaign is no longer effective for FMCG products. While email marketing in general keeps your consumers updated on latest products and promotions, drip emails in particular are a groundbreaking way to personalize your marketing tactics. Drip emails, also known as automated emails, are a set of emails that are sent to consumers based on a specific set of parameters. For example, there will be one email that is sent to consumers when they first sign up, one that will be sent if consumers add products to their cart, but leave without completing the purchase, one that will be sent after a purchase is made and so on.

Drip email campaigns are one of the most effective lead nurturing strategies. These automated mails can target consumers at a number of different stages, ultimately guiding them towards making a purchase. This technique can prove a very effective step in digital marketing for FMCG companies by helping influence the consumer decision-making process. Automated emails, which are sent when consumers abandon their shopping carts, are particularly effective, because it pushes the consumer to complete the purchase. Drip emails also help you retarget consumers who have already purchased your products. Research shows that consumers who have purchased your products in the past are more likely to do so again in the future.

6. Sell Your Products Online

While this may sound self-evident, not many FMCG products actually sell their products online. To this day, even if FMCG advertisements are being displayed on digital media, their marketing efforts are aimed at influencing the consumer's in-store purchase decision. But with the launch of many websites that let you purchase FMCG products online, an increasing number of consumers are beginning to shop online. In this case, even if a consumer intends to purchase your product, they will choose a competitor's product if yours is unavailable online. FMCG brands can choose to sell products through Amazon and Facebook or similar sites to increase sales.

Selling products online also gives you the advantage of being able to reach consumers beyond a limited geographical location. For example, a local makeup brand can start selling their products nationally by making it available online. This ultimately increases the consumer base for FMCG products, a key factor in eventually increasing sales. With a few simple steps, selling online through Amazon and other sites is a very easy way for FMCG brands to increase their online presence. For example, Raaga Professionals, a personal care brand, sells their products through Nykaa. In this way, their content marketing through blogs can direct consumers to a clear point of purchase.

7. Run Campaigns in Regional Languages

For most FMCG brands, tier II and tier III cities offer the next big avenue for growth. At the same time, most consumers in these areas are becoming more digitally connected. While the number of English-speaking users online has more or less peaked, regional language users are only going to grow from here. This has been facilitated in a huge part by the dual penetration of mobile phones and internet connectivity in India's smaller towns. A study conducted by Google and KPMG estimates that the number of non-English speakers using the internet will grow by around 18% annually. Additionally, 99% of these users will access the internet primarily through their mobile phone. For FMCG brands, this offers a huge opportunity to leverage digital marketing to attract this new wave of consumers. The growth of regional content online will be one of the key factors that can influence FMCG sales in tier II and tier III cities.

FMCG Digital Marketing Case Study: Cavin's Milkshake

Cavin's Milkshake is one of the top-selling dairy-based drinks sold by the parent company CavinKare. These milkshakes are sold in single-serving sized tetra packs and are known for their delicious flavor variants and high adherence to quality standards. Cavin's is also one of the best examples for a well-thought digital marketing strategy. With creative and engaging posts over social platforms like Instagram and Facebook, Cavin's was able to successfully utilize social media for their brand building efforts.

Facebook Posts

Cavin's Milkshake maintains an active Facebook profile, with funny, creative posts that attract a large number of comments and shares. They also have a very large, vibrant community on Facebook who actively engage with the brand by writing positive reviews on their page and interacting with their posts. Cavin's Milkshake is a staple in most school canteens and the product brings back a flood of nostalgic school memories. The #JustHighSchoolThings campaign for Cavin's stuck to the same theme, by associating the brand with school memories most people have in common. The campaign showcased the most common characters most of us were familiar with in school such as 'The Geek' and 'Cutest Couple' through Cavin's Milkshakes. These posts were very popular throughout social media, garnering a high reach and number of audience reactions. What is most noteworthy about these posts is that they have performed well organically, proving that excellent content is the most important aspect of digital marketing for FMCG companies.

Instagram Posts

Cavin's Milkshake utilized Instagram extensively for brand building. With striking visuals, their posts on Instagram were able to generate high levels of engagement from their followers. Their Instagram posts involved the clever use of popular memes, special events and engaging artwork tied in with their products. In this way, digital marketing for FMCG companies can help keep brands relevant by immediately cashing in on the latest trending topics.

Instagram was also an important channel for Cavin's to rope in their followers and build a strong community. With the hashtag #Cavin's Superstar, each month, Cavin's Milkshake showcased one of their followers and asked them a few fun questions about their love affair with Cavin's. This was an excellent social engagement technique to foster brand loyalty and encourage participation.

Influencer Marketing

Cavin's Milkshake was able to successfully utilize influencer marketing to reach moms who would ultimately purchase the product for their children. One of the key influencers roped in for Cavin's was Richa Choudhary who runs the blog 'All That's Mom.' As part of the influencer marketing campaign, Richa Choudhary wrote a blog post on Cavin's Milkshake, along with 2 social media posts on Facebook, Instagram and Twitter, plus a short video for Cavin's. These posts performed extremely well on the blog as well as on social media. Through the innovative use of Cavin's Milkshake in recipes as well as her posts on how much her child loved Cavin's Milkshake, the product developed a positive brand perception from her huge follower base.

Apart from macro-influencers, Cavin's Milkshake also worked with a number of micro-influencers on Instagram. These micro-influencers put up a number of posts where they talked about their positive experiences with the brand, used it in recipes and recommended it to their followers.

Through the innovative use of various social media platforms, Cavin's Milkshake was able to build their brand identity and reach out to their consumers.

Developing a Cross-Channel Marketing Mix

The perfect marketing mix for FMCG advertisements involves a customized combination of digital and traditional media. Developing this unique mix requires a deep understanding of your consumers. Consumers often use their phones and laptops in tandem with other forms of media. For example, they might be browsing on their laptop while watching TV or checking their phone while listening to the radio in their car. This is why digital marketing for FMCG also needs to develop strategies that effectively blend both these channels. With campaigns and FMCG advertisements that are spread over multiple platforms, brands can develop consumer awareness and influence purchase decisions.

5 Social Media Strategies to Boost Your E-Commerce Business

The e-commerce market is getting more competitive by the day and e-commerce businesses need to find unique ways to build relationships with their customers to create a loyal customer base.

For any e-commerce business, website traffic is the most important segment, yet it is the most challenging one.

Social media is playing a very powerful role today in the evolution of online shopping. It provides a platform for conversations, reviews, information and expression. An e-commerce business can leverage the opportunities provided by social media platforms for their own benefit. According to an article by Magento, 93% consumers turn to social media to help them make buying choices, while 90% say they trust recommendations from their peers.

Digital marketers have listed several strategies on how e-commerce businesses can use social media to drive traffic to their website. Listed below are five powerful tactics you can use to embrace the reach of social media for higher benefits:

Smart Targeting and Dynamic Product Ads

Leaving your ad out there in front of the masses is not such a great idea. Once you have figured out your prospective customer base, you can use targeting options provided by social media sites like Facebook to target your ads at the relevant customer base. Facebook provides you with numerous targeting options based on location, demographics, interests, device type, etc. It also provides you with features like custom audiences, lookalike audiences and retargeting. Using these targeting options, you will be able to reach your potential customers and engage them more effectively. Smart targeting will help you increase your ROI on advertising largely. Dynamic product ads can be used to retarget customers who have earlier shown interest in your products or services. To drive more sales across devices, dynamic product ads now provide a lot of flexibility and variety in functionality to e-commerce advertisers.

A classic example would be that of Cathay Pacific Airways. They used dynamic product ads for travel, to reach people who had earlier performed a search on their website. The ads featured an image of the destination city that people searched for to inspire them to act. The ads also included a "book now" button that linked directly to the booking process on the Cathay Pacific website.

Another example is that of eBay. eBay is successfully using dynamic product ads and retargeting to motivate their customers based on the customer's interest. They connect with their customers by showing them personalized and relevant products in their ads.

Facebook carousel ads are also a great way of highlighting e-commerce website products. They not only help showcase the products in detail but, when used creatively, also help drive traffic to the e-commerce websites.

Using Influencers

Influencer marketing is the new buzzword and has currently penetrated the marketing mix of many industries. Mostly food, travel and fashion are the three major industries, where influencer marketing is really climbing the ladder. Influencer marketing is a newer and more organized term for the old-fashioned 'word-of-mouth' marketing. The way people work through the buying process has changed due to the advent of the Internet and social media. People have become more efficient in their search process and they look for comprehensive and authentic information online. While associating an influencer with your business, it is important to consider the influencer's likability, credibility and trustworthiness. Remember that influencers act as brand ambassadors for the audience and thus, the information they put out there should be in sync with what the business stands for.

Influencers can be used in numerous ways: for product launches, reviews, engagement, campaigns, events and so on.

A very good example of this is the influencer campaigns done by Nykaa.com. Nykaa is an e-commerce store that deals with skincare, beauty and makeup products. Nykaa. com engages with various beauty bloggers and influencers, and weaves campaigns with them. Beauty and fashion are two areas, where people rely heavily on reviews and opinions of influencers. Nykaa leverages this very well.

Using Product Videos

The majority of online shoppers have agreed to the fact that not being able to physically touch and feel the products on e-commerce websites is their least favorite part of shopping online. This is especially true in the case of fashion and beauty industry. Product images from different angles and views may not completely explain a product's functionality or provide a proper overview of the product. Videos are the new preferred form of media and e-commerce businesses should leverage on the high acceptance of videos among customers.

E-commerce businesses can use videos to bridge the gap between offline and online shopping experiences. Product videos can help in providing a holistic buying experience to the customer and provide a clear overview of the different scenarios in which a product can be used. This makes it more appealing to online buyers. Product videos can not only be used on product pages, but also on social media feeds of e-commerce brands as well as part of Facebook or Google ads. Not only can these videos be used for Facebook and Google advertising, but they can also be used for advertising on YouTube. There are several versions of videos that are gaining popularity on social media. A few of them are live videos, 360-degree videos, 30-second videos, time-lapse videos, stop motion videos and animated or whiteboard videos.

Product videos can be used to introduce a new product and show how the product works with other similar or commonly used products from the brand and to encourage conversions from existing customers.

On1y is a food brand that caters to a very niche market segment. It provides spices, herbs and exotic seasoning. On1y uses many innovative ways to engage with its audience on social media and at the same time create a buzz around its products.

Focus on Engagement

Social media for e-commerce is not simply about pushing across products and promotions. Many e-commerce companies fail to understand this. Social media can be used very well for engaging audiences online through high value textual and visual content. E-commerce brands can find it very tempting to simply fill timelines with product promotions and advertisements. However, social media provides numerous ways by which e-commerce brands can make online shopping a delightful experience for consumers. You can engage audiences through live polls, live videos, user-generated content, contests and much more. Topical posts and festive posts can also be used to attract audience attention. To garner high levels of engagement, it is important to understand the needs of customers. Understanding this will help brands to curate content accordingly.

Social media can also be used by e-commerce brands to provide better customer service. Nowadays, a lot of customers look for solutions on the Internet and prefer quick communication over the Internet rather than going through a long phone call. At the same time, brands must encourage satisfied customers to write reviews and rate the products/e-commerce brands. Reviews and ratings go a long way in building a brand's credibility online.

Content Marketing Via Blogs and Infographics

Blogging is a great way to drive traffic to your e-commerce website. It helps your site rank higher in SEO through several internal links and backlinks. Blogging is also a good way to reach out to customer problems and be a problem solver. Most customers search for solutions to their problems online and blogging can be a great way to provide solutions to them. Long-form content helps to drive more traffic and definitely helps in higher search page ranking. Blog posts also help to subtly introduce products or promote products in an indirect way. For instance, a blog post on the topic "summer dressing" by a fashion e-commerce site could consist of summer looks using products from the e-commerce site. This will not only create attractive and useful content for the readers but will also serve the e-commerce brand's purpose of showcasing their products. Similarly, a blog post on "Top 10 budget smartphones" by an e-commerce brand like Flipkart or Snapdeal, which sells mobile phones could include descriptions of each smartphone comprising unique features and direct links to the products on the e-commerce site.

Finally, it is important for e-commerce brands to identify the right social media channels to leverage their brand. Social media platforms, if used creatively and strategically can help e-commerce businesses reach their target audience in a much faster way. The importance of social media has been adequately realized by fashion and food industries, among others. However, e-commerce brands can also leverage the benefits of social media by strategizing and creating foolproof social media plans.

Social Media Marketing Insights

Guide to Using Facebook Live Effectively

Mike Henry, a renowned writer in the media industry, once wisely said, "We're in the operating world where one good video can lead to a massive social following." With video being one of the trends to watch out for in the coming years, Mark Zuckerberg too joined the bandwagon and launched Facebook Live, allowing millions of users to gain the power to go live and broadcast themselves to anyone in the world. Going on air live is just a click away. Here is a guide to use Facebook Live effectively:

How to use it

How to go on air with Facebook Live?

All you need is your smartphone or a PC integrated with the API, the Facebook app and twelve simple steps to follow.

Step 1: Get to your Facebook profile on your Facebook app and click on the status bar like you're going to create a new post.

Step 2: To go on air, click on the 'Live' tab that resembles a video camera with an eye.

Step 3: You will find a pop-up asking for access to your camera and microphone. Allow Facebook to gain access. Once you have allowed Facebook to gain camera and microphone access for the first time, you will not receive the request again.

Step 4: Click on the 'Continue' tab on that initial page which mentions, 'Go Live on Facebook.' Clicking continue doesn't mean your video has started recording to go live. It's just a couple of steps away.

Step 5: Customize your privacy settings.

If you want your Facebook Live video to go viral and have a lot of viewers, then you could customize your audience by clicking on 'Public.' However, if you don't want everyone to view your live video and want to just keep it to your known people, you could then click on 'Friends.' You could always customize your viewers by making a specific group of audience. However, if it's your first attempt to use Facebook Live and you are still trying to get used to it and understand how it works, then you can change your privacy settings to 'Only Me.' The option to activate 'Only Me' can be found by clicking on 'More' and scrolling all the way to the end. Later on, once you are sure about your video and want it to go viral for the rest of the audience, you can change your privacy settings accordingly.

Step 6: Write a description.

Once you've got your privacy settings sorted, you will need to add in a description about the live video you will be sharing. This description will be more like a caption to the video that will best describe it for your audience. In order to gain a larger viewer list, make sure you have an attention-grabbing description so that the audience would gain interest and tune in.

Step 7: Set up your Camera View.

Just before you are all set to go live, make sure your camera is facing the right direction. You can shoot either with your front camera or with rear. You either can hold your phone vertically or horizontally, as the video will be in a square format and it will not matter.

Step 8: Click on the 'Go Live' blue button to begin broadcasting.

Once you have got all the prior steps in place to kickstart the live broadcast, all you need to do is just click on the 'Go Live' button which will then have a countdown 3, 2, 1…and the next thing you will see is you are on air going live. As soon as you start streaming and going live, you will find yourself on your own as well as others' newsfeed based on the customized privacy settings.

Your online broadcast can be as long as 90 minutes. However, do remember that the longer your broadcast is, the better the chances of a larger viewership.

Step 9: Interaction with commenters and viewers.

In order to make the most of Facebook Live, your aim has to engage with your audience by being on air and interacting with them. With Facebook Live, there are two ways through which you can interact with your viewers:

1. By speaking and responding directly to the audience through the video.
2. By having a designated person responding to the comments.

These comments and reactions can be viewed just below the broadcast live. The earlier comments will be much further down as these comments are present in the reverse chronological order, like on Twitter. While responding to viewers, if you wish to block any particular viewer, you could do so by clicking on the profile picture on the viewer's comment and clicking on 'Block.' You can always unblock a viewer that you have already blocked.

Step 10: Click 'Finish' to end the broadcast.

Once you do this, the video will stay on your timeline or page like any other video post.

Step 11: Save the broadcast to your camera roll

Once you are done with your broadcast on Facebook, you will come across an option allowing you to save your video to the camera roll like given below, so that you can always have the original copy.

Step 12: Kudos! You have officially broadcasted your first Facebook Live video. In order to review the video, you can always go back to your timeline and do so. You can also change the privacy settings, description or even delete the video just like any other post.

How brands can leverage Facebook Live

Live videos can not only help individuals post fun videos but can also help brands reach out to their audience and help build a closer relationship with their fans. When done well, these videos can be used as a medium to engage the audience and create an active conversation.

From behind the scenes videos to a product launch, this new feature is ideal to showcase some unique content. In fact, brands can also use this feature to give an opportunity to fans for an exclusive look at what's unfolding behind the scenes in real-time. For example, Dunkin' Donuts, a US-based brand did exactly that. Their first Facebook Live video was that of a behind the scenes look into their kitchen for Valentine's Day. Their fans were able to see their chefs make heart-shaped donuts. The video went viral immediately and saw great engagement and plenty of views within minutes. The video has more than 39,000 views till date.

How to analyze your performance on Facebook Live

The performance analytics of Facebook Live video is similar to that of normal videos you put up on Facebook. However, live videos do have some add-ons.

Facebook allows you to analyze a lot of metrics for the live video like minutes viewed, unique viewers, video views, 10-second views, average percentage completion, peak live viewers, people reached, reactions, comments and shares.

Apart from all of this, Facebook also lets you view and keep a check on relevant analysis of "peak live viewers" in the form of graphs for a particular piece of time during the video in order to know the interaction that had taken place.

How to access Facebook Live analytics on a business page

Step 1: Click on the 'Insight' tab on the Facebook page.

Step 2: On the left-hand side of the screen, click on the 'Videos' tab.

Step 3: To open all your videos and their analytics in a new video, scroll down and click on the 'Video Library' tab. Under the 'Video Library' window, the Facebook Live videos that were recorded will have the human silhouette icon.

Step 4: Select the video that you wish to see the analytics for and over time, you will have a graph view as well.

Want to get the most out of Facebook Live?

The following tips and tricks will help in using Facebook Live effectively:

1. Do a trial and test Facebook Live by using the 'Only Me' privacy setting.
2. If you are live, with viewers joining at different intervals, do keep in mind to reintroduce yourself and let them know what is happening so that all your viewers are in the loop.
3. Keep your video engaging and spontaneous to interact better with your viewers and get the best out of them so that they stay longer too.
4. Remember, while engaging with commenters call them out by name as it creates a better connection.

5. In order to gain more followers, go live for at least ten minutes so that your video shows up on the news feed for various other viewers.

6. Always have someone else watch over and respond to comments to make the process easier as it gets hard to reply to pop-up comments every second.

7. Don't forget to sign off by saying good bye and thank you to your audience.

8. There you go, hope this was helpful in order to understand better on how to use Facebook Live.

The Ultimate Guide to Using Instagram Stories

From being a mere selfie-sharing app, Instagram has come a long way and now has over 400 million monthly active users sharing around 70 million photos per day that garner over 3.5 billion likes daily. Instagram recently launched a new feature named 'stories,' which has a striking resemblance to Snapchat's feature of the same name. They are essentially photos and videos that last just a day and just like Snapchat, they can be made better and creative with drawings or special filters.

Stories are not part of the main feeds and are in a separate space where you can post as frequently without having to worry about spamming your friends' timelines. Wondering how to use this and how you can leverage this feature in your marketing strategy? Worry not! We have the answers.

How to use it

1. Tap the plus sign in the upper left corner of your screen to get started.
2. Take a picture by clicking on the round icon. If you are looking to make videos, press the round button continuously for 10 seconds.
3. If you don't want to take pictures and want to upload from your existing gallery, just swipe down to choose your photos or videos.

4. Once you are done with taking pictures, you can use one of the three pen options to doodle on your images.

Additionally, stories let you add filters. All you need to do is swipe right.

5. Now that your masterpiece is done, just tap the checkmark icon to share.

Your story will now appear on top of your friends' feeds. It is also visible on your profile page. You can also save this story for later use. All you need to do is open your story and click on the three dots on the bottom right, then select 'Save Photo.'

6. Get to know the analytics.

You can see who saw your pictures and videos by swiping up when seeing the photo or video. If you do not want someone seeing it, all you need to do is hit the X next to their name to block them from seeing anything you add to your Story.

You can also change your privacy settings to make sure certain people on your feeds don't get to see your stories. Go to the setting icon in your profile and choose to hide your story from select users or restrict who can respond to it.

How can brands leverage Instagram stories?

After Facebook took over Instagram, the platform opened up to advertising and more brands have started using Instagram for business. Instagram also has an in-built analytics tool, which helps you track the most viewed and liked posts, post engagement rate, website clicks and impressions.

If your brand already has a decent base, Instagram Stories is something you must quickly jump on to create a buzz. Wondering how to leverage stories? Here are a few ideas.

- **Behind the scenes**

One of the best and easiest ways to use this cool, new feature is during an event. Give your audience a sneak peek of what is going on behind the scenes. Be it a photoshoot or just a short video to show how things are working at your office. It is an excellent way to connect with your audience. Here is an example of a brand that leveraged this feature — Mercedes Benz (@Mercedesbenz) shared a collection of videos and photos of a photo shoot to showcase their new model Mercedes-AMG model.

- **Endorsing a sale**

For any retail brand or e-commerce brand, Instagram stories are an excellent way to announce a sale. With a combination of images and videos, you can send out promotional messages about your upcoming sale. In fact, J-Crew, an American multi-brand retailer did just that. Before their one-day sale of 'Jane in Pink' sunglasses, they took to Instagram stories to highlight their sale.

- **Teaser videos**

If you are having an event in your office or if you are just looking to make a big announcement about your brand, take to stories to tease your audience about it. If you are making your big announcement through Facebook Live videos, you can use stories to alert people about a Facebook Live broadcast to get more viewers for your live video. This is a great way to promote both your platforms at once.

- **Showcase your product**

If you are looking to promote your product, Instagram stories are a great way to do that. You can not only show how your product works, but also show them unique ways to use your product well. This will not only increase visibility but also give them reasons to buy the product and drive conversions. Be it makeup tutorials with a specific product or styling ideas with a scarf, there is no better way to educate your audience about your product than these stories. Even Starbucks highlighted its chilled cold brew and iced Americano with cream, using stories.

- **Celebrating milestones**

Has your company just turned one or five or did you just win a big award? Well, congratulations! It is important to announce these to your target audience and this is where Instagram Stories come in. Using a series of interview videos and images, you can create engaging content to highlight your milestone.

South West Airline is a classic example of this. When they retired their 737–500 planes, they took to stories to make this announcement. Showcasing these milestones is an excellent way to humanize your brand and keep your audience and potential customers interested in what you do and how you do it.

How to Use Pinterest for Your Brand

Building a successful marketing strategy for your business depends on choosing the right marketing mix and implementing plans that drive results. According to a recent study, marketers are expected to further increase their marketing spends this year, of which digital might consume up to 35% of their overall budgets. With digital marketing gaining more importance, it becomes inevitable for brands to think beyond Facebook and Twitter. and explore new opportunities.

Pinterest is one of the fastest growing digital platforms with more than a hundred million monthly active users, currently. This popular social bookmarking or photo sharing website allows users to create, discover and save media content related to their favorite topics, interests or hobbies, thus giving brands the perfect platform to curate relevant content and amplify it to reach the desired audience. Pinterest, along with platforms like Instagram, Snapchat and Periscope are going to be growth drivers, so try them out to stay ahead of the curve.

How Pinterest works

Have you ever enjoyed window shopping at a mall or maintained a scrapbook with clippings and articles you love or find useful? Pinterest works on a similar model where users can find, share and pin (read as 'save') visual content pertaining to a wide range of topics and interests. It allows users to create 'Pin boards' organized based on themes/topics where the pinned items get saved.

Launched in 2010, Pinterest was summarized to be a 'catalog of ideas' for people looking for inspiration. Be it a DIY project, a chocolate cake recipe or wedding gown inspiration – a wide range of visually appealing content is sourced or uploaded by users all over the web. They have also recently launched their advertising platform, which can enable promoted pins and boards.

How to use Pinterest for your brand

Big or small, businesses can use this highly visual medium to showcase expertise and disseminate content to reach a wider audience. In order to build a strong customer base and eventually some loyalty, brands can market their products and drive traffic to their website.

Pinterest is not only the second biggest online network to drive referral traffic, but also the one with a higher shelf life. Even pins that are two months old can drive a significant amount of traffic, with visually appealing images and keyword rich descriptions. In order to effectively use Pinterest to build your brand and achieve marketing goals, please find below some tips:

1. Set up your account

With the growing user base and average time spent on this platform, Pinterest seems to have become the new favorite for marketers around the world. In order to get started on this platform, sign up for the business account that provides exclusive features to help you grow and monitor results.

Your business name, category, website and bio are all you need to create your presence on Pinterest. It provides analytics, rich pins and advertising in terms of promoted pins, which are not available otherwise. In case you already have a personal account for your business with good fan-following and referral traffic, Pinterest allows you to convert it into a business account without losing any data.

2. Plan your approach

Visuals are the most powerful medium for brands to capture the attention of its target audience and communicate better. Good and compelling visual elements tend to perform better for brands and result in higher engagement.

Retail brands should showcase relevant, high-quality and vertical images of their products for users to like, repin or follow your account for more. Even brands with intangible products or services can benefit from Pinterest with the right content and strategy in place. Businesses that belong to healthcare, finance, education and other sectors can creatively modify their existing content into visual elements or share new content that is relevant to their business and target audience.

3. Create boards and pins

It is ideal to start with 8–10 boards with content categories that are relevant to your audience and business. Instead of just promoting your own products and speaking the brand language, look for relevant keywords or topics that are most searched by your target audience. Curate content based on user interests and create boards for broad themes and categories.

With Pinterest being the second largest social network to drive referral traffic, make sure you pin images, videos or infographics with links to your website. These backlinks can be included in the descriptive copy or photo caption for higher click-through rates

4. Boost your SEO efforts

Use the right keywords and hashtags in your descriptions and image titles to get noticed and gain more traction. In order to create quality backlinks and visits to your social media handles, add these links to your profile and individual pins that will drive traffic. Much like other platforms, local businesses can tag their location to pins and profiles to reach relevant audience on Pinterest. You can also see some of our other link-building techniques and tips here.

5. Make your website or blog Pinterest-ready

Pinterest is a great platform to discover new products as it caters to a wide range of categories such as fashion, home décor, art, food, gadgets, travel, etc. Marketers can add a 'Pin' button to their products on the site to make it easier for visitors to share it across. For e-commerce players or businesses that sell online, these pin buttons can help in generating more sales and traffic.

Engage with your audience

In order to be easily discoverable as a brand and engage with your audience, repin relevant content across Pinterest and create group boards. This enables brands to invite bloggers or influencers to contribute to different themes and ideas. It also helps in building a community and interacting through contests, theme boards or by liking/commenting on their repins and personal collections. As Jeff Bullas mentions in his article, Shopify users referred by Pinterest spend an average of $80 compared to Facebook referrals of $40.

How to Use Instagram for Business: A Guide on Instagram Ads

Instagram's growth and spread as a social media platform is a tech fairytale. What started out as a purely recreational app by two young entrepreneurs is now nothing short of a global phenomenon. It's been a couple of years since Facebook acquired Instagram and now the platform has an estimated 400 million monthly active users. After Facebook's acquisition, Instagram has opened up advertising opportunities on its platform making it official that Instagram is truly a powerful marketing platform.

However, if you plan to use this platform to market your brand, product or service, you must be aware that the regular, run-of-the-mill content and strategy will not work for Instagram. If done well, Instagram can not only increase your brand's visibility but also can help you engage with your customers and generate business and revenue through it. So, here's a list of ways to use Instagram effectively for your business.

You are what you click

Instagram is a very visual platform and therefore you have to use images and videos that can tell your brand story effectively. Use high-quality product images but use the images to showcase your product and not to sell it. The pictures must look organic and as natural as possible.

Ensure that your captions are brief yet engaging. Adding a question always helps to interact with your audience.

You can share plenty of behind-the-scenes pictures and videos that can let people know about the team that works for the brand. Remember, the more real you are, the better people connect to your brand.

Once your Instagram profile creates this fun, creative and organic atmosphere, you can start seeing an increased traffic to your site and curiosity about your product/service.

Bio and website link

Unlike Facebook and most other social media platforms, Instagram does not allow clickable links on the posts or in the post description. However, the profile bio allows you to write a brief about yourself or your business. Use this space to convey exactly what you would like to say to your audiences. Most brands also use a few emojis here to make this section stand out and support the text with some color.

The website link added here is the only way your customer can be redirected from Instagram to your website (other than ads).

To subtly push your target audience to engage with your website, blog or your app, end most of your post content with a gentle reminder that the link to reach you is available in the bio. Check out this post by Photo Concierge, showcasing stock images directing customers to a link of their choice.

Instagram ads

As of March 2016, there are over 200,000 advertisers on Instagram and it's a great tool to reach your target audience. Since Facebook owns Instagram, you will need to go through a Facebook Ad

Social Media Marketing Insights

account to run ads on Instagram. Here's a quick guide on how to run Instagram ads:

- Visit the Facebook Ads Manager and create an account. Skip this process if you already have an ad account with Facebook.

- Link your Instagram profile to your page using the tab under 'Settings' on your business Facebook page.

- Select your goal from the options that are offered through Instagram. For instance, you can send people to your website, get people to download your app or promote your Facebook post through your Instagram profile.

Clicks to Website
- Send people to important sections of your website
- Available Ad Formats: Photo, Video, Carousel

Website Conversions
- Get people to take specific actions on your website
- Available Ad Formats: Photo, Video, Carousel

Mobile App Installs
- Get people to install your mobile app
- Available Ad Formats: Photo, Video, Carousel

Mobile App Engagement
- Get more activity on your mobile app
- Available Ad Formats: Photo, Video, Carousel

Video Views
- Tell a story using video
- Available Ad Formats: Video

Reach and Frequency
- Achieve predictable reach and greater control over message frequency
- Available Ad Formats: Photo, Video, Carousel

Page Post Engagement
- Get people to engage with your ad
- Available Ad Formats: Photo, Video

Mass Awareness*
- Drive mass awareness to a broad audience with guaranteed impressions and placement in the top ad position of Instagram's feed
- Available Ad Formats:

- As of now, one cannot promote a post on Instagram unless it is shared on Facebook.

- Now create the ad on the Facebook ads manager with the image and text of your choice.

- When you reach the ad format section, you will have the option of deciding if you would like to show your ad on Instagram. Alternately, if you would only like to run your ad on Instagram, make sure you uncheck the other platforms.

- Now fix your budget, check the ad preview, hit 'Place Order' and you are good to go!

✓ Desktop News Feed	Remove
✓ Mobile News Feed	Remove
✓ Instagram	Remove

Please select media for your ad

✓ Audience Network *ⓘ*	Remove
✓ Desktop Right Column	Remove

Like any platform, you need to experiment with various combinations of ads and text to understand which ads are working well with your target demographic. Try the carousel format with multiple pictures or a video ad to get the desired business results.

It has been observed that running Facebook ads along with Instagram ads can reduce your cost per conversion by around 20%.

Engage and reach out

Engagement with your followers is quite hard on a platform like Facebook, but Instagram is the perfect place to really engage with your followers. It's also a place that is geared more towards organic and real conversations.

Your followers are a gold mine of potential customers. Creating a loyal fan base is a sure-fire way to generate customers. Of course, unlike running ads, this process takes a bit of time, effort and patience.

Sorting and keeping in touch with followers is vital. Tools like SocialRank are a fantastic way to organize, manage and identify your Instagram followers.

SocialRank essentially pulls out the profiles of all your followers and lets you sort them out based on your preferences. You can create lists of your most valuable followers and ensure that you follow them back. A thoughtful message on their special posts can go a long way in ensuring brand affinity.

Another interesting way to grow your community is by searching relevant non-followers and liking as well commenting on their posts. Richard Lazazzera, author of *What to Sell Online: The definitive guide*, ran a small experiment wherein he shortlisted 100 of his competitors' followers and liked as well commented on their posts. He managed to get a whopping 34% follow back from this group.

Follow: 14% follow back

Follow + Like: 22% follow back

Follow + Like + Comment: 34% follow back

This clearly shows that the more effort you put into your Instagram profile, the better your chances to build a strong and relevant community, which in turn helps with business results.

Another great way to engage with your users is by reposting customer content. Most brands heavily rely on this and it's a great way to make them feel special. Use the Repost app to share your customer's content and tag them in the post! In fact, there are many tools that help you manage your Instagram profile.

Keep your account clean

Instagram is a platform where often, unfollowing is as important as following!

Since following others is a definitive way to increase your reach, you have to constantly unfollow the people who do not engage with you in any way. Some accounts that you follow may have become inactive and can be weeded out.

Crowdfire is the perfect app to help keep your account clean. Through its simple dashboard, you can quickly see the number of people who follow/do not follow you. It also pops up the profiles of your recent unfollowers, which can help you unfollow them as well. Alternately, it helps you to quickly find the list of your competitors to follow. With this dashboard, you can ensure that your account is always fresh and updated!

Hashtag your way to glory

We all love hashtags. We are all guilty of using them all the time. But nowhere are hashtags more important than on Instagram. You can use up to thirty hashtags per post and we recommend using it well. The hashtags can be broadly divided into three categories

- Popular Hashtags (#tbt, #photooftheday, #igers #popular).
- Industry Related Hashtags (#Fashion, #FoodPorn, #instatech, #FitnessFreak).

- Brand Related Hashtag (#Vogue, #UberCode, #MyntraFashion).

Ideally, each post must have a few from each of these categories. Do not forget to coin a hashtag for your brand and promote it regularly till it can catch on and have its own identity among your customers.

Many brands also use clever hashtags to communicate an emotion or trend related to their product. Just like this Starbucks post, where they use the #BeGoodToYourself hashtag along with their tea to indicate a feeling of wellness and indulgence.

Instagram influencers

Instagram influencers are very powerful and have almost the same impact as a popular brand ambassador for your business. Anybody who has a large following and content that interests your customers can be an influencer.

The key to getting the most out of influencer marketing is ensuring that it is done using several influencers and within a short time period. Your customer's memory is short and to ensure that your brand is noticed, a 'Blitzkrieg' approach to influencer marketing can go a long way. This is especially true when you are launching a new product in the market.

One of the best case studies to understand the impact of Instagram influencers is the launch of the Uwheel, a self-balancing two-wheeled hoverboard. The co-founder's girlfriend recruited famous rappers, singers, socialites and other Instagram influencers to talk about the Uwheel, all at once. Some of the posts and reviews were paid for, while some others were given the Uwheel in exchange for a word about their business and product on their profile. And suddenly, the Uwheel was all everyone was talking about!

Using a marketing budget of $61,200 their team was able to generate revenue of over a million dollars and since then, Uwheel as a brand has not turned back.

Analyze this

Like all social media platforms, Instagram analytics can help you understand your account and follower behavior to help optimize your business. Using tools like Social Insight or Iconosquare you can find out more about important analytical points. For instance, the best time to post your content, most engaging content, most engaging filters etc.

These tools help generate comprehensive reports that can speak volumes about the user behavior and help you understand what works and what does not for your Instagram account.

Post regularly

With Instagram, consistency is very important. You must keep sharing your content in different forms to be relevant and sustain the community you have built. One way to achieve this is by scheduling your posts in advance. Use tools like Schedugram and Latergramme so that your workload does not stop you from posting regularly on Instagram.

However, do remember that the name Instagram is inspired from the act of capturing a moment the instant it happens. Nothing works better than taking a picture as it happens and sharing it immediately with your followers. A successful sales figure, a new product launch, a new business venture – share it when it takes place! During a recent interview, Eva Chen, Instagram's Head of Fashion Partnerships, speaks about how Instagram is more than just a numbers game and airbrushed photographs. Even grainy, but real, videos that were taken in poor lighting can do well on Instagram if they truly capture real life. So, don't be afraid to share it all.

Here Is Why You Should Use Linkedin in Your Marketing Plan

LinkedIn, over the last few years, has come a long way from being just a job search portal to a platform for lead generation, especially for B2B and small business. The platform has globally around 500 million users and 42 million Indian users, making it an ideal platform to promote your content. However, with Facebook having a sophisticated advertising platform and ad formats, more marketers preferred Facebook for lead generation. Understanding this, LinkedIn recently introduced changes to its advertising methods, making it a comprehensive platform to generate leads. Here is a look at all the changes that marketers need to know:

If you have used the Facebook Ads Manager, using the LinkedIn advertising platform will not be too difficult.

Why LinkedIn ads work

- **Creates awareness about your brand**
- **Reaches decision makers** - From CEOs of fortune 500 companies to senior level executives, LinkedIn has all the top decision makers who can potentially see your advert.
- **Increases the reputation of the brand**

LinkedIn lead ads

The LinkedIn lead ads is the coolest and newest update that the platform has introduced. It is also the most useful one for any B2B business. You can use the LinkedIn lead forms for your sponsored content and campaigns. It works like a regular ad but when you click on the call to action, it takes you to a pre-filled lead from within the platform, making the entire experience seamless and hassle-free for users. The form is pre-filled because the form already extracts most of the information from the user's profile. With more marketers going the mobile first route, this ad format is an excellent option to explore, especially since it does not take you to a landing page or a website, making the process much faster and easy to navigate on the mobile.

Here is a guide on how to create the lead form ad:

Step 1 - Select the Lead Forms option

Go on to the LinkedIn advert manager and select the preferred language, type the name of the campaign and choose the ad format as, "Collect Leads Using LinkedIn."

Step 2 - Choose the content

Choose the content that you would like to promote. You can choose from the available content that you have posted or post new content for your target audience.

Step 3 - Set up the lead form

The next step is to set up the lead form. Enter a form name, a headline and other information needed. Treat it as a landing page and give all the necessary information including a powerful call to action to make sure that the user fills out the form.

Step 4 - Choose the fields for the form

The next step is to create the form and you can choose up to seven fields that you want to collect from your lead form including name, email address, job title and phone number.

Step 5 - Thank you message

You also have the option to set a thank you message and display a URL that can take the user to a landing page or website, once someone fills out the form.

Step 6 - Select the target audience

Selecting the target audience is the most important step to collecting the right leads. LinkedIn gives you the option to choose from a wide range of them based on demographics, job titles, location, industry, skills, gender, etc. Once you have selected the audience, choose the budget and define your bid type from CPC or CPM and voila, your ad is now ready!

Measuring results from the Lead Forms

Apart from giving you the basic information of the cost per lead, LinkedIn also tells you how many people opened the advert, how many of them opened the form and how many submitted as well. You can also download the leads from your form and use that data for future campaigns.

Matched audience

LinkedIn already has detailed targeting options, which allows marketers to target potential audience by company, job title, etc. However, the platform has now expanded and introduced a concept called matched audience. Matched audience lets you retarget website visitors and add your contact database. This option gives you the chance to target people who are familiar to your business, giving you a better chance of capturing the lead and driving sales. Using matched audience, you can target.

Website visitors

As the name suggests, with this feature, you can target people who visit your website. Make sure you add the LinkedIn pixel on all pages of your website, just like how you add the Facebook pixel and create custom audience in the tools section of campaign manager.

Contact targeting

If you have a database of your customers, with contact targeting, you can add them to your LinkedIn campaign manager and target them.

Account targeting

Account targeting lets you reach powerful people who call the shots within your target accounts. All you need to do is upload a list of target companies to match against the 8+ million company pages on the platform.

InMail ads

Sponsored InMail ads look just like a regular email and present the opportunity to marketers to send personalized messages to their target audience. The InMail ads act as an email marketing campaign which is sent to the target audience's LinkedIn inbox, without having to acquire their email ids. The best part about this feature is that it has 100% delivery as the emails are sent only to people who are active on the platform when it is being sent.

InMail ads are a great way to showcase your product, branded content, webinars and promote content downloads such as e-Books and infographics.

With the Sponsored InMail ads, you can target a variety of target audience relevant to your business just like the lead ads.

The ads are only sent to a user once in 60 days so it eliminates the question of spam and crowd.

Best practices for creating InMail ads

- Keep the subject line catchy
- Personalize your greetings and your target audience by using their first name
- Use compelling text and visuals
- Use a powerful call to action
- Use relevant target audience

Who should advertise on LinkedIn?

With more than 500 million users and various ad formats, LinkedIn has become the go-to platform to promote content. If you are a small to medium size business and want to sell to decision makers, LinkedIn is the perfect place to be. According to data, more than 80% of the leads generated for B2B companies come through LinkedIn. From promoting relevant content to showcasing the product, B2B services can create a niche market for themselves on LinkedIn.

Although LinkedIn is synonymous with B2B sector, we have tried it out for B2C sectors as well. It especially works well for real estate, education, finance, publishing industry, etc. With the right targeting, a business can increase their visibility and possibly generate leads. Given below is an example of how one of our real estate clients, Mahindra Lifespaces, leveraged LinkedIn lead ads to improve the quality of sales. To promote one of their properties on GST Road, Chennai, they look to LinkedIn lead ad feature to target senior level executives. The ad opened to a lead form within the platform, gives a convenient way for potential investors to contact the buyer. With LinkedIn, Mahindra Lifespaces saw a 5x increase in leads at about 20% of the cost.

The Ultimate Guide on Brand Marketing via Snapchat

A picture speaks a thousand words, a phrase that we are all familiar with. Snapchat, a social media messaging app, proves this phrase right. Similar to Instagram, Snapchat allows users to share pictures and videos for a set amount of time with friends after which the picture self-destructs. Evan Spiegel and Bobby Murphy launched it in 2011. It is widely popular amongst teens and young adults. This trend is starting to gain momentum amongst other generations as well.

How to Use It

Download the app

The Snapchat app is available on both Google Play and App Store. Begin by downloading this app.

Set it up

Once you have downloaded, the next step is to sign up. Set up your account by entering your email, a username and a password. However, it is advisable to choose a good username since Snapchat, unlike other apps, does not allow you to change your username once you set it.

Account settings: Adjust your privacy settings. To do this, click on the ghost icon on the top part of the screen. This will lead you to the settings tab in which you can choose who can view your snaps and stories.

Profile picture: Snapchat lets you set an animated profile picture. Tap on the ghost icon on top of your screen and click on your snapcode. Then, upload a picture of your brand.

Look for friends and customers

Now that you are all set, it's time to connect with your friends. To add a new friend, click on the ghost icon and then select 'add friends,' this lets you add customers or brand well-wishers either from your address book or by username or snapcode. You can also add fans by location.

Send snaps to your fans

To share a snap with your fans, open the camera and click on the circle button present on the bottom of the screen. You can also shoot a video for which you would have to press and hold the button a little longer. You can also enhance the snap by adding filters, texts and images on it.

The latest Snapchat version offers you a variety of lenses that are fun to experiment with. To use this, click and press on the screen, this would allow it to capture the shape of your face. Once this is done different lenses appear and you can choose and try different ones by scrolling left.

After you are done, you can send the snap by tapping the arrow in the bottom left side of the screen.

Share story

A snap story can be viewed by everyone on your friends/fans list. You can add multiple snaps and videos and this stays for twenty-four hours.

Follow the same steps as creating a snap, except instead of choosing few people to send it to, you need to choose 'my story' to post this.

Live chat

This feature on the app allows you to video chat with your fans. To start a video chat, click on the video button present below the chat tab. This can be an interesting way to showcase a new product launch or to talk about a new/interesting development with your brand.

The emojis

Snapchat has different emojis next to your contacts to denote the different levels of friendships, which is based on your Snapchat activity. Be careful while using this for your brand as these emojis also needs to represent the tone of not just your brand, but the message being amplified.

How to Use It for Your Business

Snapchat is one of the fastest growing social networks. This medium helps you to come up with some fun, engaging and creative campaigns. The app's features like filters, geo filters, adding text, emojis, etc. add the element of fun to snaps. Many brands have begun to use Snapchat as a part of their marketing strategy. Wondering how you can use Snapchat for your business? Here are a few ways you can:

Live events

If your business is hosting or is part of an event, use this app to cover all the live happenings at the event. This way your audience members will be able to view your event live, no matter where they are.

MTV-VMAS Celebrity Story

Channel MTV created a live story during the VMAS, where they were updating snaps live from the event. They received around 12 million views on this platform. All the fans, no matter where they were, could view everything that happened at the award show.

Behind the scenes

Take your fans behind-the-scenes. This is a great way to engage with your audience and get them excited. Capture some fun moments at work, like celebration, team lunch, etc. Experiment by using all the features of this app. This gives the users a different experience from what they would get from other social media platforms, which in turn, will make them, want to engage with your brand on this platform.

Once the users get a glimpse of what is going on behind the scenes it will make them feel like they are a part of an overall process.

Contests and offers

Just like other social platforms like Twitter and Facebook, you can host fun and exciting contests on Snapchat. You can use this medium to provide the promo code for a sale that is happening in your store or website. This is part of the shopping trend and seems to have worked well with a few brands.

Influencer campaign

In today's world, influencer marketing is one of the popular ways to reach a wide target audience. Tie up with influencers that have a high Snapchat score and a good number of followers on other social media platforms as well. Influencers who are avid Snapchat users will know of ways to make the content even more interesting by using all the features of the app. Disney World hired Mike Platco, whose personal account gets close to 120,000 views per snap, as an influencer when they launched their Snapchat account. Mike is a great storyteller as well as an artist and he utilized these skillson his snaps that were taken around the theme park.

Demonstrate your products

Launching a new product? Create a buzz around it and get your fans excited and geared up for your product launch. Give them a sneak peek or a preview of the new product.

Apart from product launches, many brands make use of this platform to give a demo of their products.

Burberry leveraged this medium to feature their new collection before the actual show early this year. This way the brand was able to increase the engagement with its fans by getting them geared up and excited for the actual show.

Geo filters and sponsored lenses

Create and add geo filters for your brand. Sponsored geo filters work well for many brands. Since this lets you add your logo or anything specific onto the filters. Sponsored lens is another interesting way to engage the audience. This helps in terms of branding as well.

Beats, the famous headphones company, used a sponsored lense to promote their black Friday sale. Users were able to add the lense over their photo to create funny videos in which the user's eyes would get wide and their heads would move back and forth.

If you are not using Instagram or Snapchat for your business, you are missing out on something! So, go ahead and start exploring ways to leverage these platforms.

Advertising

The Ultimate Guide on How to Advertise on YouTube

Consumers are spoilt for choice across multi-devices and multi-channels, thus making sales competitive for marketers. As consumers become more and more digitally sound, marketers constantly feel the need to evolve and source new ways to reach their relevant audience to drive long-term online sales. This has lead marketers to venture out and capitalize on brand and product videos, along with text and display ads. Here is an ultimate guide on how to advertise on YouTube, types of ad formats, the best way to optimize and measure results for your campaigns.

Why Is It Time for Every Brand to Experiment With Video Content?

Videos are entertaining, engaging and help increase customer retention.

As per Google, there are only two things users do more than watch videos: sleep and work. Every day, people spend hundreds of millions of hours on YouTube and generate billions of views. Users consume videos to feel the rush, laugh, connect and learn. The youth, the younger generation and tech-savvy users are on YouTube most of the time through their mobiles, thus making this channel the most preferred media platform on the go. Studies also claim, 42% use YouTube for pre-purchase research and 64% buy products after watching a video on YouTube, making videos the future of entertainment and online marketing.

Fusion Between YouTube and Video Ads

YouTube, being the second largest search engine is a powerful media mix to retain old customers, gain new customers and engage savvy customers through video content.

YouTube is also a community-driven social media channel that values genuine content and meaningful engagement with real people and stories. To get the most out of YouTube, the video content and ads need to build a relationship with YouTube users above and beyond the traditional advertiser-customer relationship.

Since consumers' purchase decisions are influenced by the video content, promoting content with advertising messages can make it difficult to increase viewer engagement with the brand.

Videos that are light, fun, humorous, emotional, real and true make it through to the consumer's heart and mind.

Be Spoilt for Choice – Multiple Video Ad Formats on YouTube

To advertise on YouTube, there are several video ad formats and each offer a unique opportunity to attract consumers and achieve goals. Before making an ad, it is prudent to have a clear marketing goal and know the audience to reach them in the most cost-effective way.

The Ad Formats

TrueView in-stream ads – skippable video ads

Skippable ads are designed to capture the attention of the relevant audience in the first five seconds of the video. After five seconds, the audiences are given a skip button, to skip the ad and continue watching their initially selected video. These are excellent ways to increase visibility on cost per view as YouTube charges only after the ad is watched for thirty seconds or more. Skippable YouTube ads appear on YouTube watch pages right before, during and after other videos and to top it all, give free visibility for the first few seconds. These ads contain a call-to-action button that often links to a landing page.

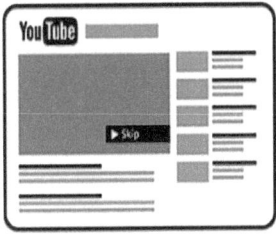

TRUE VIEW IN-STREAM ADS - SKIPPABLE VIDEO ADS

Skippable ads work best for branding and often have a lower conversion rate. Although these ads are best for people who view similar content on YouTube, avoid targeting by keywords as this could significantly limit the frequency of the ads. Create an engaging video in the first five seconds to keep viewers from skipping the ads.

TrueView in-stream ads – non-skippable video ads

They are similar to In-Stream video ads, but viewers do not have the option to skip them. The ads usually play for 15–20 seconds and up to 30 seconds. Non-skippable YouTube ads also appear on YouTube watch pages right before, during and after other videos. Viewers have to view the entire advertisement. They work best when videos are short, simple and showcase good offers.

TRUE VIEW IN-STREAM ADS - NON- SKIPPABLE VIDEO ADS

Bumper ads

Bumper Ad formats are designed to increase brand awareness and impressions as well as reach a wider audience. They are usually non-skippable short video formats of six seconds or shorter and play before, during or after another video. Advertisers are charged on impressions (cost-per-thousand-impressions).

BUMPER ADS

TrueView discovery ads/in-display ads

These ads appear in the top-right section of the YouTube search results page and to the right of the feature videos. They also appear below the player (for larger players) and are meant to capture the attention of the viewers while watching other videos. They blend with organic listings. They have a thumbnail image with a short copy and the advertisers are charged when the viewer chooses to click the thumbnail and watch the ad.

TRUE VIEW IN-STREAM ADS - IN-DISPLAY ADS

The images on the thumbnails make first impressions and need to provoke the viewers to click and watch further. Choose the video still that highlights the content the best. Also, try and match the image to the content in the promotional text or keywords.

Display ads are best suited to increase subscribers rather than directing them to the landing page.

YouTube in-video overlay ads

As the name suggests, these ads are semi-transparent and appear in the lower 20% portion of the watch video space on YouTube. Link the call-to-action to the relevant landing pages as these ads have a higher chance of lead conversion.

YOUTUBE IN-VIDEO - OVERLAY ADS

With these ad formats, advertisers can advertise their ad inside the videos of their competitors. Overlay ads work well as they get more views without causing interruptions.

Video Optimization and Best Practices for Video Ads

Try these tips to optimize your YouTube videos and keep your viewers engaged for long:

Link AdWords account and YouTube channel

Link AdWords and YouTube to allow both the networks to work together and provide deeper insights like click and engagement performance, reach and frequency, video viewership as well as other advanced data and reports.

Try the KISS theory – Keep it (the video ad) short and simple

Hook viewers in five seconds. Create engaging video content to elevate your customer's video experience to get more viewer engagement.

Communicate the brand/service clearly and provide a strong call-to-action button to guide the viewers to the next process i.e. make a purchase, visit a landing page, subscribe, like, share, comment and so on. Having a clear call-to-action within the ad helps direct traffic from the ads to your YouTube brand's channel or website with additional video content.

Deliver the most relevant message when the video begins, so the audience gets the crux of the video content, in case viewers plan to skip the ads after five seconds.

Use the remarketing list to define the audience

The demographics and other details help to venture into a new platform.

Creation of relevant playlists based on search

YouTube uses play time or watch time, a factor in the algorithm, to suggest videos and create playlists which can be used to boost the overall play time of your videos. When the next video automatically starts playing at the end of the first video, there is a higher probability of keeping the viewer longer on your page.

Use Call-to-Action for subscription in the video to enable more channel subscribers and engagement

YouTube has a feature to create 'Subscription Links' that asks the visitors who click on the link to subscribe to the channel before playing the video. This can help gain more subscribers for the channel, thereby boosting the long-term reach and engagement. This is how many brands have grown their subscriber base.

Be open to comments from the viewers

As they say, any publicity is good publicity. While you receive comments and criticism, it is also important to respond to the viewers.

Targeting and Reaching the Right Audience for the Content

YouTube has a potential to reach a vast audience. YouTube is the world's second most-used search engine and the third most-visited site after Google and Facebook. It has a total of 1.3 billion users and three hundred hours of new video is uploaded every minute.

By targeting video ads on YouTube, advertisers can reach relevant customers on the spur of the moment, just when they are interested in a particular product or service. YouTube's varieties of targeting options help reach the right customers when it matters.

Advertisers can use contextual placements to show ads on specific videos, channels or websites – places that attract audiences with a high conversion potential. Advertisers can also target by keywords, interests, placements, remarketing lists, location and demographics – age, gender, and parental status.

Advertisers can also place their ads on their competitors' videos and steal leads from right under their noses.

It is not only the volume of users that make advertising on YouTube so interesting, but also the nature of the platform and how audience interact with videos and the brands.

Cost of Video Advertising

The cost of making a video depends on the subject, message and its length. It also varies from one brand to another. But advertising on video can be completely controlled and measured. An advertiser can spend as per his/her convenience and only pays when someone engages with the video ad or watches the video for thirty seconds or more. There are also other ways to optimize your AdWords and YouTube campaigns.

Tracking and Measuring Results

YouTube's easy to use in-built analytics helps advertisers monitor the performance of the video ads and channels. Data like demographics, watch time and traffic sources help the advertisers to optimize the campaigns further. Advertisers can make adjustments to the ads at any time and also are free to run multiple ads at once to see which works best.

Google AdWords also provides certain key metrics to analyze the ad performances in detail. Want to increase leads and multiply your revenue? Log into the AdWords account, click on 'Add New Campaigns,' select online video and start creating your campaigns. Remember, the call-to-action button must make viewers click the ads and optimizing the video ads is the key to better results.

The Most Definitive Guide to Optimize Your Adwords Campaign

Every business big or small, belonging to any category is now using digital marketing to help their business grow and reach the masses. Internet marketers know that Google AdWords is an excellent way to drive traffic to a website. Setting up an AdWords campaign is not just about making ads and running them but also getting the best results for the amount invested.

So, how are the best results obtained?

The best results are obtained when the campaign is set up properly (Check out our Definitive AdWords Campaign Launch checklist) and optimized properly on a regular basis. Therefore, optimizing your AdWords campaign is important. If not managed properly, it can prove to be expensive for the business.

Optimizing an AdWords campaign is the most complex task, as every aspect of the account like click-through rate, poor performing ads, using correct keywords, average cost and much more, need to be analyzed. The optimizing process is continual and will have to be paid constant attention to in order to maximize revenue and gather sufficient data about the account performance.

Here are a few tips to optimize your Google AdWords account at different levels of the account:

Campaign Level

1. **Checking on bid adjustments:** Bid adjustments allow you to show your ads more or less frequently based on when, where and how people search. Bid adjustments are set by percentages which can be either increased or decreased.

   - **Mobile bid adjustments:** Depending on the number of clicks and converted clicks, you can increase or decrease your mobile bid adjustments. As the image below shows, since the conversions from mobile are higher, the mobile bid adjustments have been increased by 50%.

   - **Location bid adjustments:** If a campaign has no location selected, the ads will show on all locations. To avoid unwanted impressions and clicks, always select the location before the campaign is live. Location bid adjustments help you decide which locations you want to focus more on, based on their performance. As the image shows that conversions are higher in Greater London, the bid has been increased by 25% making your ads appear more frequently.

Location	Bid adj.	Clicks	Imps.	CTR	Avg. CPC	Cost	Avg. Pos.	Conversions	Cost / conv.	Conv. rate	All conv.	View-through conv.
Greater London, England, United Kingdom	Increase by ▼ 25 %				£2.04	£4,213.87	1.4	130.00	£32.31	6.32%	130.00	0
60.0 mi around (51.507350,-0.127758)	Example: A £10.00 bid will become £12.50				£1.94	£2,003.51	1.3	69.00	£29.04	6.68%	69.00	0
Surrey, England, United Kingdom	Save Cancel				£2.02	£335.94	1.5	14.00	£24.00	8.43%	14.00	0
Hertfordshire, England, United Kingdom	Setting multiple bid adjustments? Here's an example: United States × Saturday = Result +20% (1.20) -5% (0.95) +14% (1.14)				£1.90	£275.59	1.4	11.00	£25.05	7.59%	11.00	0
Berkshire, England, United Kingdom	--	123	1,777	6.92%	£2.09	£256.78	1.4	9.00	£28.53	7.32%	9.00	0
Buckinghamshire, England, United Kingdom	--	98	1,566	6.26%	£1.89	£184.74	1.5	4.00	£46.18	4.08%	4.00	0
Suffolk, England, United Kingdom	--	64	928	6.91%	£1.91	£122.45	1.4	4.00	£30.61	6.25%	4.00	0
Thurrock, England, United Kingdom	--	6	106	5.66%	£1.79	£10.74	1.7	1.00	£10.74	16.67%	1.00	0

2. **Search v/s search partner networks:** Check how ads are performing on the other search network partners with Google. If conversions are less you can always go to the all settings tab and choose to not show ads on other Google search networks. By clicking on that option, your ads will not show on other Google networks.

3. **Top v/s others:** By selecting the top v/s others option under the segment tab, a table with statistics appears showing where your ads appeared on the Google search top (above the organic search) and otherwise (below the organic search).

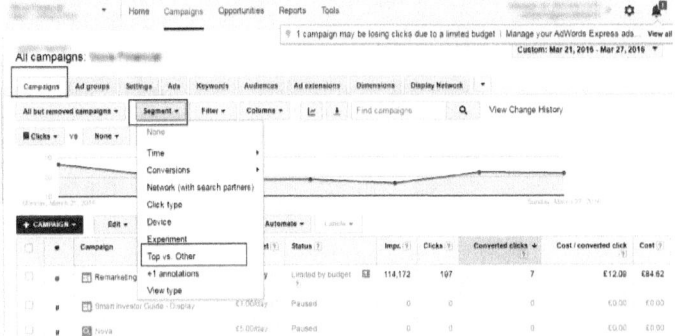

The below image depicts that conversions are higher when the ads are on top, so to always remain above the organic search one can increase their CPC and get higher conversions.

Similarly, sometimes being below organic search i.e. "Google search other" shows higher conversions than Google search top. In this case, you need not bother about increasing your bids to be on the top.

4. **Ad schedule:** By adjusting the ad scheduling bid, you can show your ads on specific days and also at specific times. At the campaign, click on the Dimensions option and see which day's ads conversions are higher. Based on this data, adjust your ad bids.

The below report shows that conversions are higher on Saturday, Sunday and Monday. Based on which the ad schedule bid adjustments have been increased so that ads appear more times on those days, leading to higher conversions.

Day	Clicks	Imps.	CTR	Avg. CPC	Cost	Avg. Pos.	Conversions	Cost / conv.	Conv. rate	All conv.	View-through conv.
Tue, Aug 4, 2015	43	5,200	0.83%	£2.54	£109.42	3.6	0.00	£0.00	0.00%	0.00	0
Wed, Aug 5, 2015	66	4,250	1.55%	£2.40	£158.22	3.7	0.00	£0.00	0.00%	0.00	0
Thu, Aug 6, 2015	64	4,224	1.52%	£2.49	£159.56	3.4	6.00	£26.59	9.30%	6.00	0
Fri, Aug 7, 2015	59	3,968	1.48%	£2.55	£150.55	3.7	3.00	£50.18	5.08%	3.00	0
Sat, Aug 8, 2015	58	2,947	1.97%	£2.60	£150.61	3.6	9.00	£16.73	15.52%	9.00	0
Sun, Aug 9, 2015	59	2,689	2.19%	£2.63	£155.30	3.2	5.00	£31.06	8.47%	5.00	0
Mon, Aug 10, 2015	62	4,332	1.43%	£2.58	£160.22	3.8	12.00	£13.35	19.35%	12.00	0
Tue, Aug 11, 2015	60	3,190	1.88%	£2.59	£155.17	3.2	5.00	£31.03	8.33%	5.00	0
Wed, Aug 12, 2015	56	3,116	1.80%	£2.86	£160.42	3.7	4.00	£40.10	7.14%	4.00	0
Thu, Aug 13, 2015	62	3,082	2.01%	£2.54	£157.44	3.3	10.00	£15.74	16.13%	10.00	0
Fri, Aug 14, 2015	53	3,672	1.44%	£2.84	£150.68	3.3	5.00	£30.14	9.43%	5.00	0
Sat, Aug 15, 2015	53	3,065	1.73%	£2.82	£149.38	3.4	6.00	£24.90	11.32%	6.00	0
Sun, Aug 16, 2015	55	2,473	2.22%	£2.76	£151.92	3.0	13.00	£11.69	23.64%	13.00	0
Mon, Aug 17, 2015	56	2,941	1.90%	£2.88	£161.16	3.5	9.00	£17.91	16.07%	9.00	0
Tue, Aug 18, 2015	70	3,835	1.83%	£2.29	£160.60	3.4	7.00	£22.74	10.14%	7.00	0
Wed, Aug 19, 2015	62	3,563	1.74%	£2.54	£157.42	3.6	5.00	£31.48	8.06%	5.00	0

Day and time	Campaign	Bid adj.	Clicks	Imps.	CTR	Avg. CPC	Cost	Avg. Pos.	Conversions	Cost / conv.	Conv. rate	All conv.	View-through conv.
Sunday - all day	Smart Investor Guide - 1	+15%	407	5,757	7.07%	£1.57	£640.22	1.0	33.00	£19.37	8.13%	33.00	0
Monday - all day	Smart Investor Guide - 1	--	380	6,232	6.10%	£1.76	£670.48	1.1	13.00	£51.58	3.42%	13.00	0
Tuesday - all day	Smart Investor Guide - 1	--	372	5,092	7.31%	£1.83	£682.41	1.1	23.00	£29.57	6.20%	23.00	0
Saturday - all day	Smart Investor Guide - 1	--	371	4,290	8.65%	£1.67	£619.89	1.1	38.00	£16.19	10.33%	38.00	0
Wednesday - all day	Smart Investor Guide - 1	--	370	5,060	7.31%	£1.70	£628.76	1.1	27.00	£23.29	7.30%	27.00	0
Thursday - all day	Smart Investor Guide - 1	--	310	4,805	6.45%	£1.79	£556.25	1.1	23.00	£24.18	7.42%	23.00	0

Ad Group Level

- **Pause poor performing ads:** For an AdWords campaign to succeed and meet the business goals, you need to regularly review and refine your ad's performance. Ads with high conversions and CTR are performing well and ads which do not have conversions and CTR are not performing well. Such ads can be paused.

- **AB test ads:** AB test ads basically mean that in the same ad group you have the same ad with different variations. The elements of variation could be: ad text, the negative keywords for the ads and different landing pages. This AB test ad method will help you see which variation is performing better. Based on the data, the other ads can be paused or changed.

Keyword Level

- **Pause unproductive keywords:** At the campaign level, choose the keywords tab and click on the download button. This keywords performance report will give you the details on how each keyword is performing and what is the average position, converted clicks, CTR, cost, clicks and impression. Based on the statistics from the report, pause keywords that are expensive and have less or no conversions and CTR.

- **Improve keyword quality scores:** The quality score of any keyword depends on the ad relevance, expected CTR and the landing page relevance. So, to improve the quality score for your keywords, ensure that your ads have relevant keywords in them and that keywords are grouped correctly to ensure relevant ad copy is served to users.

- **Add negative keywords:** A search terms report shows the keywords customers are searching for. Based on this report you can either add or exclude the keywords at the campaign, ad group and the ad level.

- **Manage keywords bids:** When you select each keyword, you choose how much you are willing to pay. This is known as the keyword's maximum cost per click. Based on how your keywords are performing you can increase bids for better performing keywords – keywords with large conversions and low-cost per click.

UX & Web Design

How UX Can Break or Make Your Business Sales or Revenue

Understanding user experience and its importance

The father of UX, Don Norman, defines user experience as a science that encompasses all aspects of the end user's interaction with the company, its services and its products. User experience takes more than just defining it. Let us relate it to the real model.

What makes shopping fun? Most of you would say, 'buying the product.' I agree, but not entirely. Buying the product is the last step of the shopping process. What led to buying is your positive experience at the store, walking down the different sections stacked with a variety of designs and then finding the perfect take away. Not to forget, the billing experience!

Let us map a real-world model of your online experience on a business website: reaching a website through a certain landing page, reading the content, navigating the site and finally taking a conversion action; everything counts as user experience.

Research studies on UX and A/B tests on websites have led to pointing out thrust factors that impact the experience of a user on your website.

UX Factors that lead to conversion

Let us see below why product pitch, good navigation and aesthetic content form the crux of your website:

1. Product pitch

The pitch of a website sketches out the business identity. Content that speaks out about how the business goals are intended to benefit their customers, caters positively to the user's experience. This is the part of experience, where the tone of the website builds trust and communication with the user. A strong selling pitch can boost your sales.

2. Comfortable and intuitive navigation

Comfort and intuitiveness are key factors that lead a user to conversion. Even if you perfectly speak out about how good your product is, if a user fails to see the interface as friendly, intuitive and quick – they are likely to bounce.

3. Content and aesthetics

Neil Patel says that great content is definitely the reason behind returning visitors and he quickly adds that good content is valuable only when it's readable and engaging. That's where aesthetics comes in. Content becomes friendlier, when the formatting stands out in a way that grips the user's attention. A good use of contrast colors for backgrounds and text can make a piece of content interesting to read, adding images that are crisp and meaningful makes your content ten times better, visual cues using text formatting, colors and icons can guide the user about your site.

Everything that brings about a conversion like important content, call-to-action, contact information, etc., should be made to stand out by using principles of aesthetics.

In addition to SEO, Google algorithm emphasizes on returning results that have an excellent user experience. So, it's important to always look back at how your website is doing from the UX perspective.

Here is an excellent example to demonstrate how the thrust factors contribute to providing an experience that builds a trusting relationship between the customer and the product.

Gehna, a brand that sells stunning unique Indian jewelry, have made their online presence valuable by providing a user-friendly platform for online shopping and jewelry customization.

Some of the reasons why Gehna's landing page user experience ticks:

1. The first impact this website makes, is with its aesthetics. Clean layout with enticing images, interesting fonts and color balance, which ultimately lead to a pleasant experience.

2. The content on this page is kept optimum without distractions and has excellent customer value. Studies in cognitive psychology state that a user is prone to action whenever he finds all the necessary information around a CTA. The banner on this page impresses the user by laying out their available services in a dignified way. This is the point which engages the user and leads to conversions.

3. By giving their users an insight into their work, customization process and user testimonials, they have built their trust with their prospective customer.

The World of Gehna

4. They also maintain a user-friendly blog with design ideas and jewelry trends. This shows that Gehna is not just a business, but also a work of passion for customer interest, thereby bringing out the personality of their brand.

To sum it up, with their unique propositions, well-organized content and evident CTAs, they have provided the customer an impactful experience that bags conversions. I urge you to remember, a great landing page UX leads to the quickest conversions.

If you notice in entirety, it's the little things that tend to add up in a big way. What demonstrates this is the power of a well-designed form with a prominently placed CTA.

Every CTA leads a step closer to conversion. Once a prospective customer decides on a product/business, the only thing in between is the experience of making it happen. Be it a registration, purchase checkout or a reservation – more often, the last step towards a conversion is completing a web form. UX is indeed impactful here.

To understand this better, let's take a look at a few insights from *ConversionXL's Peep Laja*.

- **Less information request = more conversions.**

The key is to ask only for relevant information and skip the research questions. This means that a five-field form out performs a nine-field form by approximately 30%. Research studies based on usability ROI has seen that every time a form was simplified, businesses saw huge increases in their conversion rates.

- Provide necessary information on the form. Missing information leads to confusion, frustration and no conversion.

With a great service pitch, an eye-catching image and simple fill-out form, Pamperazi clearly tells you what you're up to.

UX is so impactful that it can break or make your business revenue

Statistics from experiments conducted by various organizations has shown the tremendous impact that UX has had on sales/revenue. Let us explore a few examples and case studies.

Call to actions

According to Jared M Spool, founder of user interface engineering, changing a CTA button on a checkout form increased a major e-commerce website's annual revenue by $300 million. In fact, studies even show that a prominent CTA button right next to some related content can increase conversions from 2.78% to about 19%.

Here is a great example of Casagrand Aldea. It adds prominence and proximity to the CTA.

1. Providing sliding images of the exteriors and interiors of the apartments.
2. Displaying the amenities and perks of the apartments, evidently.

Having given a perfect picture of what the user is signing up for, a CTA is provided right in place for users to make further enquiries. This is a high-converting UX.

Visual design

A well balanced design is about proper use of page elements and colors. Visually balanced designs have a positive impact on the user experience.

LaundryBoy is a winning design that puts together a great visual balance. With their website themed around blue shades, they have made their CTA completely stand out in a balanced contrast. Would you ever believe that a visually balanced design could lead to a 25% higher conversion rate?

Practice of de-cluttering

Your landing page will always face a five-second test to grab the user's attention. The impact made here brings about the conversion. The Weather Channel wanted to turn people into premium subscribers. They de-cluttered their homepage and had a single subscription action with their features enlisted.

Listen to the users' voice

Users, be it retained customers or prospective customers, have come into the habit of letting businesses know what is causing the friction. Valuing their feedback yields a huge difference in your conversions.

Creating a new sign up page based on user feedback raised the revenue for SEO Moz by an additional $1 million.

Your users are adapting to trending designs, which is why your designs have to update as per contemporary standards or be even better.

With a great UX, make them an offer they can't refuse

A lot of research has been done around the impact of design on content. Recent studies on cognitive psychology state that people are moving from text-driven content towards visually mediated content.

Content is stronger and easily assimilated when accompanied by informing design/images.

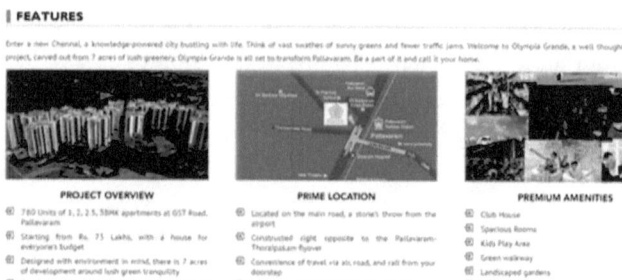

Olympia Grande makes the right use of content and images to showcase the strength of their residential project. By placing prime information like project overview, cost and enquiry in a compact space of the user focus, they have got the user's attention. That is a winning strategy for quick conversions!

UX impacts SEO, which in turn impacts your sales

A good UX makes your website accessible, useful, usable, findable, credible and valuable. All of this impacts the SEO positively, leading to a good ranking on search engines. A website that is optimized with quality content and good experience will gain customer traffic and succeed at customer retention.

It is wise to learn from others' mistakes; it is a faster path to move ahead. Bad UX is mostly about doing the basic functionalities wrong. So, in addition to demonstrating what works, let me point out what does not.

Common Issues in UX that break sales

- Slow loading time of websites
- Lack of content hierarchy
- Cluttered and confusing navigation
- Lack of basic functions or information that a majority of the users expect

- Exhaustive user engagement for simple tasks
- Falling short of an impressive personality
- Lack of responsive design

Research studies in UX have shown that 88% of the visitors do not visit a website that has given them a bad experience.

As you see, UX is an integral part of a business website, bridging your customer to your business. Understanding the usage pattern of your users gives an insight into their experience, learning what part of your website frustrates or confuses them helps incorporate some necessary changes to the website to get better conversions.

With a lot of companies investing in UX, it is evident that the user's experience with a website has a soaring impact on the sales and revenue.

Here is wishing your user experience good health!

How Design Can Help Tell a Brand Story

"Once Upon a Time…"

Those four words, when combined, either embrace nostalgia or a magical moment about to be told…a story!

Storytelling has been prevalent since the days of cave writings. However, as mankind progressed, new technologies emanated and with superhighways of online interactions, brands are constantly swimming against a ferocious tide of customer attention. In a world, where information is prevalent, visual design aids to strategize further by informing, engaging and delighting the audiences.

Good content and narrative make a story alluring, but a story viscerally explained and duly designed with the right tone, signals and aesthetics amplifies the content, converting an ordinary experience into an extraordinary experience. That is the power of visual storytelling!

Having said that, how do we strategize design in our brand's narrative?

According to a study by Visual Teaching Alliance, 90% of information transmitted to the brain is visual. A logically thought out visual design strategy with the right elements of photos, graphics, colors, type and videos swiftly connects the customers with the brand's key values, garnering engagement to its true potential. However, a logical balance must be maintained in design as undue over-telling of the story may boomerang, affecting the brand otherwise.

Here are some tips to help you jump-start your visual storytelling strategy

- **Embrace visuals**

The human brain processes visuals 60,000 times faster than text. The magic is truly in the innovative use of images that reflect authenticity, cultural relevancy and real-time human experiences. This nurtures cascading effects amidst viewers by fermenting emotions and engagement to the story.

Most of the real estate and travel brands, for example, use visuals and images to their advantage by taking their customers on a perspective tour of their products, amenities and the surrounding facilities. See how we leveraged the power of photography to take the consumer through a visual journey around the globe.

- **Use infographics effectively**

Infographics are a great way to compile information and present it in a visual and digestible format to tell a story about your brand's journey. Infographics with compelling visuals and factual information ensure that the content goes viral and enables analytical tracking while also magnifying you as an expert.

- **Set your color palette**

Colors have the power to pitch different moods and brand values, as well as increase brand recognition by up to 80%. When used effectively, your brand's color palette can evoke emotions, nurturing your story. Are you a fun brand that wants to inspire creativity and youth? Then you may want to consider vibrant and fun colors. However, if you are a serious brand built on trust, you may want to use trustworthy colors. Playing with the same color over and over across all channels steamrolls to build a better brand connect.

- Choose your colors in order of importance — primary color, the one which you want to be the primary voice of your brand, to the secondary palette (the ones you will use the least).
- Choose colors that are functional and ensure good contrasting tones.
- Use images that harmonize with your color palette.

For example, notice how Google uses the primary color palette (red, blue, yellow and green) across all its imagery to reflect its playful and innovative culture.

- **Determine your brand's fonts**

The choice of fonts you choose also affects the way audiences perceive your brand and its personality. Consider using two to three fonts consistently in all channels; one for the title that should be expressive of the brand's persona along with another easy-to-read font for the subtitle and the body copy.

UX & Web Design

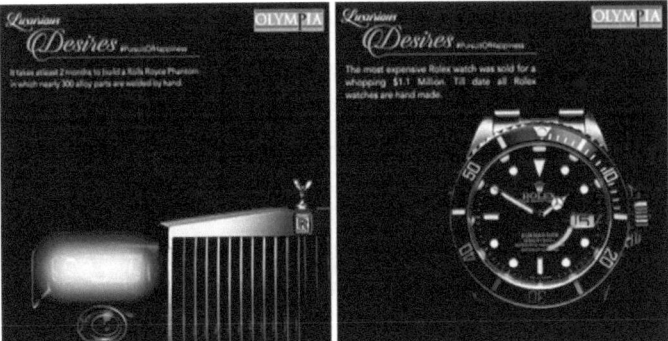

Olympia #PursuitofLuxury series

In the #PursuitofLuxury series we did for a luxury real estate brand, Olympia, notice how we paired a sans serif font for the body copy with a script font for the title to add to the premium feel of the brand.

- **Elevate with the right filters and effects**

Enhancing images with tints, vibrancy, saturation, hues or blurring will set the mood for the story giving it a unique look/feel that can reinforce the brand's culture. Most importantly, the filters must have the same synchrony to other elements as per your style guide.

Take a look at how we used the vintage time-lapse effect to illustrate how luxury transcends time.

Olympia's #LuxuryTranscendsTime series

- **Keep the brand layout consistent**

Ensure the position, size of logo, tagline and other brand visuals remain consistent. While using them over images, ensure that it can offset against its background.

- **Templatize to get recognized**

Creating templates for campaigns will efficiently brand a story. Notice how weekly recipe posts on social media by On1y, a gourmet herbs and spices brand, has a similar format, which includes the brand colors, fonts, title, images and name. Such consistent elements tie each post together rousing the campaign's cognizance.

- **Personalize your strategy**

Embrace the special features, capabilities and audience demographics of videos, Vine videos, GIFs and memes to foster different types of engagement.

The Vine video by Dunkin' Donuts, where coffee and lattes represent football players, is a fine example of how vine videos can be used to garner viral status.

- **Give it a human touch**

Adding a name and face in the form of characters or mascots to your brand story adds life to the narrative, ensuring authenticity.

A simple cartoon, illustration, hand sketches or animated short films can highlight the storyline while also sharing information about your brand.

In an innovative way to communicate the company's heritage, Murugappa Group compiled a series of live sketches with the hashtag #SayingItSimply videos, followed by a social strategy designed to foster engagement.

- **Spice up your brand's online presence**

The timeline cover photo provides for a good amount of real estate to capture due attention from social media followers like Twitter, Facebook, Pinterest, etc. The online social space provides for a good amount of real estate to visually pitch your brand story.

The power of design in storytelling is no fairytale. The race to get customer attention is on and your brand's visual voice is what will get your brand noticed.

Content Marketing and SEO

Content Marketing v/s Native Advertising

- *86% businesses now leverage content marketing in one form or another.*
- *70% audience wants to learn about products via content instead of direct advertisement.*
- *More than 67% clients ask their content marketing agencies about native advertising.*

Outbound and interruption marketing is losing its sheen in favor of content marketing and native advertising. Though they seem similar, there is quite a difference between the two forms of marketing.

What is content marketing?

Content Marketing is a marketing approach that involves creating valuable and useful non-promotional content by brands. The important part in the first sentence is "valuable and useful." Self-serving and promotional content cannot be placed in the content marketing bucket: value-add is the only secret.

Goals of content marketing

The goals for content marketing can be broadly categorized:

- Educate your potential customers
- Create brand awareness
- Generate qualified leads

- Long-term and effective Search Engine Optimization
- Establish thought leadership

Different forms of content marketing

Content marketing can be done in varied formats but some of the key ones are discussed here:

- Videos are one of the most engaging forms of content on the web. The consumer web video traffic is expected to reach 80% by 2019–2020. For a long time, video marketing was considered a game for the big brands. But of late, this trend has been broken with small businesses and start-ups leveraging the medium to showcase excellent meaningful content. OYO Rooms launched a video on the occasion of Independence Day that garnered more than 3 lakh views in a couple of days. The *Madras Song* by Murugappa Group was launched as a tribute to the city of Madras on the occasion of Madras Week. The video stole the limelight during the 375th anniversary celebrations of Madras.

- Blogs are an excellent way to build an engaged audience, showcase your company as an industry thought leader and at the same time boost search engine rankings. According to a recent HubSpot Survey, regular blogging boosts lead generation by 126%. It also provides fresh, unique content to your website, which is an important factor considered in Google search rankings.

- Infographics are graphics that showcase long content in a visual and interesting manner. Our brain absorbs and processes visuals faster than any other form of content. Hence, infographics as a form of content can be a great way to showcase information and make your blog more engaging.

- SlideShare and case studies are other fascinating forms of content marketing. These are more suited for B2B businesses. Companies are looking out for specific information and if your case study or a SlideShare can help fit into the gap, you will gain a relevant mind space among your potential customers.

- Relevant and Informative social media content can go a long way to help create an engaged community of potential customers. Innovative and clutter-breaking content can help your brand quickly carve out a niche on social media. Petwish – a startup in the pet food space, did an interesting content series around different dog breeds in India. The content quickly became viral among pet lovers across India, which was an excellent audience for the brand.

- Podcasts or audio telecasts are possibly one of the most underrated content marketing tactics. It gives you access and visibility to a different audience who is tuned to short content in a format that allows them to multitask "on-the-go." For example, a motivational podcast while on the way to office in the morning or solid investment advice from an avid investor that will help you plan your investment strategy for the coming week.

Metrics to track the effectiveness of content marketing

- Number of shares and likes
- Number of backlinks/mentions to your content
- Number of leads

Tips for an effective content marketing strategy

- Identify the needs of your target audience
- Create 10x content – make it better and more thorough than anyone out there
- User-generated content needs to be a part of your content strategy
- Content amplification is important – creating content alone won't help until it reaches the right audience
- It's a long-term game so do not expect quick-fire results

What is native advertising?

Native advertising is a form of paid advertising, where the content put out seems similar to the native content of the platform. You would have come across one or the other form of native advertising daily – while reading an e-newspaper, browsing through an e-commerce portal or on your favorite Google search engine. According to *Business Insider*, the global native advertising spend is estimated to cross $21 billion by the year 2018.

Goals of native advertising

- Increase brand/product awareness
- Supplement content marketing in amplification
- Drive traffic to your website or landing page
- Boost lead generation and sales

Different forms of native advertising

- Content recommendations are one of the most prominent forms of native advertising. You would have seen sections at the end of news articles under the title "Recommended Articles" powered by recommendation engines. These native ads are done via platforms like Outbrain, Taboola and Content.ad.

- Influencer marketing is a rapidly growing form of native advertising. Under this, the influencers and bloggers talk about your brand or product on their blogs or social media channels with a backlink to your online property. The articles are seeded along with other articles on the blog.
- Search engine ads are those that surface on top of your search results. This form turns out cheaper than other forms of native advertising, based on the CPL or sale.
- In-feed ads are presented within the list of natural articles from the publication. Though these ads are well-blended within the native experience of the reader on the platform, they are marked as sponsored ads for the benefit of the customer.
- Promoted listings are the product listings that show up on top of the category page on e-commerce websites.

Metrics to track in native advertising

- Reach or impressions
- Clicks or traffic to your website/landing page
- Leads or sales
- Cost per Click
- Cost per Lead

Tips for native advertising

- Create separate landing pages for different native ad ideas. The hook to get people on your landing page and the content on the page need to speak the same story.

- Research your audience well to create and experiment with multiple hooks to see what works well for your audience.
- Make it interesting. Only bragging about the brand doesn't work anymore. Show the content and convince the reader that you are the one who can deliver the experience or service to the user.
- Do not shy away from allocating a good budget for this to show results. The CPL or sale from native advertising is traditionally higher from content marketing.
- Do not use native advertising for SEO. There is no SEO takeaway from this exercise.

What Type of Content Will My Target Audience Find Engaging?

Content is King, a statement that has held true since the dawn of advertising. Like all great things, content marketing has evolved and improved over time. Gone are the days when brands would simply pin-up posters of their products in any given location to try and entice consumers.

Take the above ad for example. Published in 1958 by David Ogilvy's company, the ad created a sensation among Americans of that era and greatly increased the sales of Rolls-Royce. Reading it today, you may find it hard to skim past the long content, but Ogilvy utilized one of the most powerful elements in advertising that is still held in high regard today: Audience Engagement.

He did so by using a powerful headline that was able to connect well with the emotions that the target audience felt at the time (the posh society of post-war America). Flash-forward to over six decades later, Ogilvy's methods of engagement are still applicable, but have been morphed to fit into the current scenario of an internet and technology-savvy world.

Content marketing is an advertiser's new best friend; 71% of consumers today feel bombarded with ads on social media. Instead, they want more than just a flashy product commercial; they want an experience, a little taste of what to expect. Content marketing can achieve that by creating and distributing valuable, relevant and consistent content. The method also adds a layer of trust in the target audience, creating what brands crave the most — loyalty towards their products

Why must you implement a content marketing strategy?

Leads/Sales from a long-term perspective

The fact that content marketing gives you an open playing field to mix and match with various content forms over a multitude of platforms means there is a big chance for your brand to generate leads, improve sales conversion and ultimately get closer to your target audience on a more personal level.

Reach consumers who use ad blockers

Everyone hates a pop-up ad. They are annoying, they disorient you from an online experience and are generally considered spam. Content marketing provides a more genuine, trustworthy advertising approach, one that actively induces consumer interaction.

Get organic traffic/SEO

Without SEO, anything you publish online will be lost forever in the massive sea of stars that is the World Wide Web. Content marketing has proven to be an SEO-friendly marketing method and provides credibility by boosting organic traffic.

Ad fatigue

Imagine seeing the same ad over and over again as you scroll through your Facebook feed. It can get annoying to the point where consumers lose interest in what the ad is trying to communicate. With content marketing, marketers can keep the essence of the ad fresh while varying the way the ad is presented.

Popular content forms in use today

Infographics

Self-explanatory in its naming, infographics is the presentation of data in a visual way. The concept is widely popular among readers and gives license to creative freedom in graphical presentation, adding loads of value to the written content. Being a more comfortable way to consume information from, infographics are three times more likely to be shared on social media than general content posts.

Memes

Short and sweet; memes are one of the easiest content forms you can make. But bear in mind that they are not used for information, rather for entertainment. If done right, memes have a high chance of going viral, as consumers love nothing more than to share something outright hilarious.

Videos

If a picture is worth a thousand words, then videos are worth a million. No matter what you are promoting, there are always ways to present it on screen. Videos have proven to be one of the most searched forms of information or entertainment, so to give your SEO a big boost, consider making one that is relevant to your brand, product or service.

Guides and e-books

Guides are a detailed form of content and specifically meant for sharing information. Guides work well for SEO purposes as Google's crawlers are now paying more attention to long-form content that mixes and matches with other content forms.

Book reviews

There is a book for everything today and your target audience is bound to pick up one. Avid readers will love to know how good a book is before they have a read, plus it gives off the impression that you are well-versed in your subject matter, adding a layer of credibility to your brand. You can induce some consumer reaction by asking for personal reviews.

Product reviews

Like books, product reviews will boost your brand's credibility and if you engage professionally with service providers and manufacturers that are relevant to your industry, that credibility increases tenfold. Collaborate with influencers who can review your product and add a trust factor among consumers.

"How-to" posts

The age-old 5Ws (Five Ws) and 1H (how) concept is still effective to date and a "How to" post is something that is frequently searched. If you are SEO hungry, "How to" posts will help generate the same, as the format takes advantage of long tail keyword searches, ultimately bumping up your site ranking.

List

Humans are hardwired to be obsessed with lists. If you make one relevant to your product or service, chances of it being read are very high. Lists are everywhere and can comprise anything. Google analytics have revealed that numbered lists (odd numbers count) are the most popular.

Case studies

Nothing spells professionalism better than a good old case study. Need to explain what your product or service is and its impact on consumers? Perform a case study with all those intricate details. Ultimately, you will get a healthy dose of credibility and if promoted well, a strong consumer following.

Podcasts

The radio may have lost its charm among the general audience today, but audio files still hold high regard among commuters who like a good plug-and-play of useful information. If your target audience falls under such a category, podcasts could be a useful medium for some knowledge sharing.

Remember, there is no hard and fast rule that you must try every form of content marketing. Instead, focus on adapting and implementing an idea into a select content type. When that idea morphs into a quality piece of content, your target audience will evolve from one-time consumers to a dedicated and loyal fan-following.

Platforms on which content marketing thrives

No matter what type of content you choose to work with, you will need a base, a platform on which your content becomes viewable. In the online world, content representation can be divided into three types.

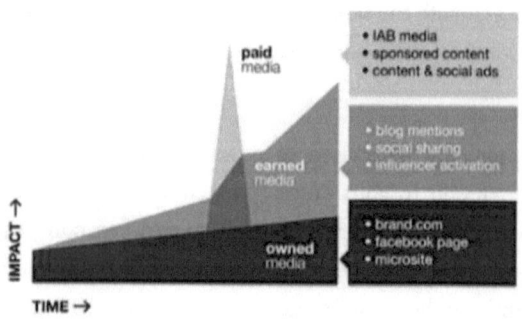

Source: NeilPatel

Paid Media

Media that is bought and sold — online advertisements like Google AdWords, Facebook ads, YouTube ads and sponsored content have shown a very high percentage regarding reach towards the target audience and are also reliant on ROI. Strong reach may increase the chance of a targeted user getting convinced to purchase, yet may not provide a longer, more sustainable impact that permanently etches your brand into the consumer's memory.

Owned media

Owned media refers to platforms through which your content is promoted. Your website, Facebook page, YouTube profile, LinkedIn, Twitter and Instagram accounts are types of owned media. Think of owned media as your virtual office, a space for you to actively promote everything your brand represents and connect to your target audience in the online world. Since owned media is just a platform, you are free to use it in any way you like for your content marketing needs. How effectively you use it, with your chosen content strategy, will determine the overall reach and interaction with potential consumers.

Earned media

Even if your brand is marketed well online, consumers need to be certain and feel a sense of trust with your product. You can achieve that trust factor through earned media; sharing of social media content, Twitter mentions, blog mentions, product reviews and influencer marketing. Of course, to gain such high level of trust among consumers takes time, but also pays off handsomely in the long run, immensely boosting your brand loyalty.

The content marketing formula

Content marketing isn't something you could just cook up out of an empty pot. The process requires careful planning and meticulous detailing with a whole host of ingredients blending to make fantastic pieces of share-worthy content on various platforms.

The basic formula

Content Marketing = Ideation + Creation + Publishing + Promotion

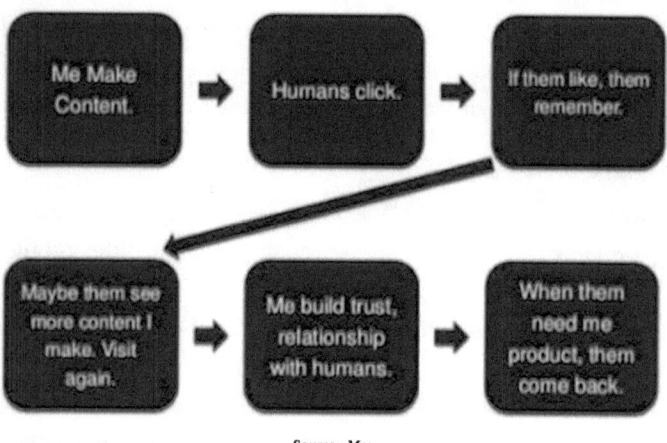

Source - Moz

Ideation

Everything begins with an idea. It is from this seed that your entire content marketing plan branches out. To come up with a path-breaking idea, you need to do research and lots of it at that. You achieve great content marketing, when you bridge the gap.

"What they're looking for"- Analyzing your target audience

This is the first and most critical step towards creating your content plan. When you can understand who your audience is and what their expectations are, you will be able to create more relevant content. Analyze these aspects:

- Audience demographic (age, sex)
- Audience geographic (location)

- Audience behavior (reactions towards competition brand's content)

When you narrow down the points mentioned above, your next step is to hunt for relevant topics that are trending, valuable and share-worthy and in some way link to your brand, product or service.

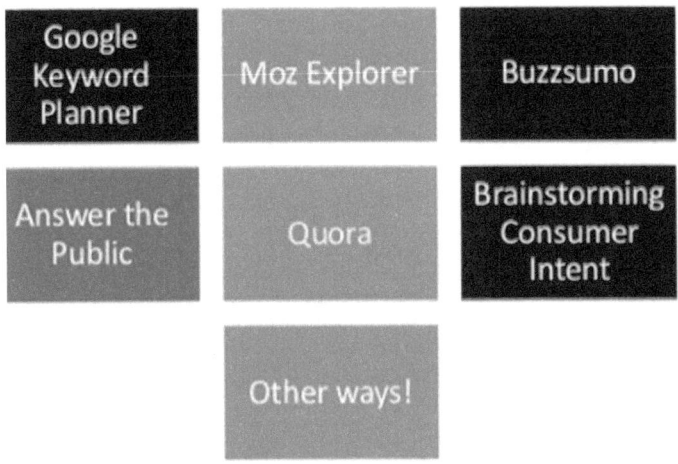

"What we want to say"- Create a content strategy

Question yourself as to why you are about to create a piece of content. What is your end goal with the content you are about to create? To make this easier and more understandable, create a content strategy. Your strategy must be able to answer one or all of these goals:

- Boost brand awareness
- Increase brand reach
- Page promotions
- Boost website visits
- Focus on consumer interaction

Remember, strategies could change even after your content is created and published. Be open to a trial-and-error method before you push for massive promotions.

Creation

With your strategy set and your ideas in full flow, it is time for the actual creation of your content. Again, depending on your target audience, your type of content will have to vary, but make sure you stick to a content formula that is valuable, relevant and has great visual appeal. Based on current market trends and audience expectation, keep your content fresh by mixing and matching various forms like GIFs, blog posts, infographics, videos, etc. Ultimately, your content creation must sync well with your strategy and be able to:

- Solve a problem
- Trigger a purchase decision
- Add value to SEO
- Entertain

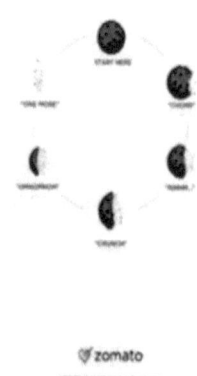

Publishing

Much like creating content that relates to your target audience, publishing your content must also have a timed approach.

Google Search algorithms and Facebook's targeted post boosting have made it easier for marketers to preselect a publishing time and date, resulting in better and more accurate reach to the consumers. It is important to optimize content that is shareworthy on mobile devices as well, with a majority of consumers now spending more time on smartphones.

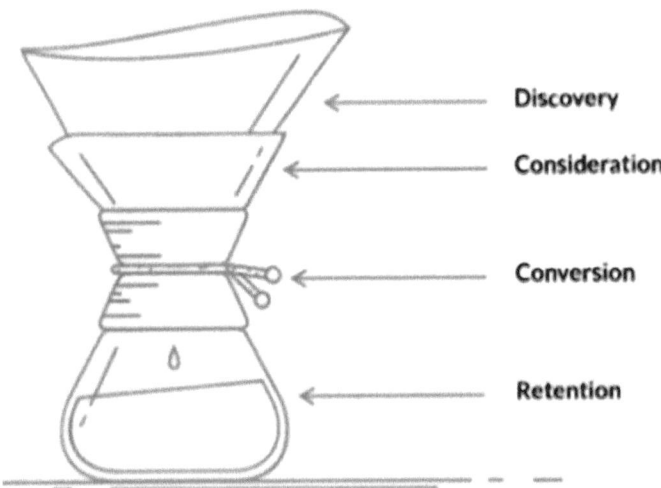

Different content is required at different parts of the funnel

- Discovery
- Consideration
- Conversion
- Retention

Promotion

With over 27 million pieces of content being shared every day, your content is just a small grain of sand in a huge desert. To make that little grain noticeable among the rest, you need to make the most out of the promotional options available.

So how do you amplify your content?

Promote on Social Networks especially Twitter, LinkedIn, Slideshare	Use LinkedIn Ads, Facebook Ads & Promoted Tweets	Notify your email list
Respond to questions on Quora, Reddit, comment on blogs, take part in industry forums	Reach out to people who have shared similar content	Leverage the reach of influencers

Remember, none of these techniques will work wonders unless you connect them with the golden catalyst of content marketing — Search Engine Optimization.

Brand/Product/Service specific content marketing

Since content marketing is an ever-evolving subject matter based on shifting trends and change in consumer behavior, there is no sure-fire successful approach to choosing an approach to your strategy. But, some content strategies work well over others depending on your brand, product or service. Let us look at a few successful strategies.

Content marketing for B2B

When it comes to B2B content marketing, ultra-professionalism is important. Your task as a marketer will be to convince other businesses to work with you or use your services. Make sure your content is concise, to the point and expresses your services and the benefits it could offer to another business.

Best platforms

Facebook, Twitter, LinkedIn, WordPress Blog/Website, YouTube and Google AdWords.

Content type

Emailers, Helpful blog posts (Tips/How-to), Product Reviews and Product/Service specific social media posts.

Content marketing for FMCG

For FMCG brands, the content strategy must heavily revolve around consumer interaction. This means marketers are free to explore all sorts of content and modify them in a way that involves consumers' intrigue and curiosity to know more about the brand's products.

Best platforms

Facebook, YouTube, Instagram and Guest blogging.

Content type

GIFs, Memes, Influencer promotions, Product-specific social media posts and Guide-based blog posts.

Content marketing for real estate

With a recent influx of the real estate market in India, developers are making a move into the online space to boost their project promotions further. As always, the competition is fierce, so the best reach towards consumers decides the big winner. Considering how huge the real estate industry is, having an online presence for developer and broker, while also complementing each other's presence is vital for the success of a real estate brand in the online space.

Best platforms

Facebook, Google AdWords, WordPress blog and Twitter.

Content type

Emailers, Helpful blog posts (Tips/How-to), Influencer promotions, Product-specific social media posts and Landing pages.

Content marketing for lifestyle brands

Lifestyle brands, especially those in the fashion industry, have a mainstay in the digital marketing space. To get better online presence, lifestyle brands must be appealing both to targeted consumers and businesses.

Best platforms

Facebook, Instagram, Google AdWords, WordPress blog/landing page, Twitter and YouTube.

Content type

Emailers, helpful blog posts (tips/how-to/lists/guides), influencer promotions, product-specific social media posts and video promotions.

We end by quoting a famous line by David Ogilvy, *"Never write an advertisement which you wouldn't want your family to read. You wouldn't tell lies to your own wife. Don't tell them to mine."* Content marketing is the most trusted and honest form of marketing and one that is sure to go a long way in establishing a healthy relationship with your target audience.

Content Amplification Strategies to Effectively Promote Your Content

Creating high-quality content is important, but the buck doesn't stop there. If your content is share-worthy, you need to cook up an amplification strategy that creates an impact across various channels. Sharing your content is not enough; there are over 27 million pieces of content published on a daily basis, so whether you are writing a business article or a casual article, your content needs to be spruced up to stand out in the crowd. Here are some nifty content amplification strategies that will promote your articles, if used effectively:

Respond to questions on Quora

Quora is recognized as the most comprehensive and trusted online forum. You can ask and answer questions relating to any subject matter. Since forums provide an open source for your target audience to discuss a topic, you can add value by responding to their queries using your existing write-up, if relevant. You can also link back to your blog or website, which effectively renders your work as a credible source.

Use LinkedIn Pulse to republish your article

LinkedIn is the most effective networking site for both established organizations and enthusiastic start-ups. All top-end professionals in the management level have active profiles on LinkedIn and are always on the look out for interesting information relevant to their industry. Publishing your blogs on this platform will elevate the reputation of your organization as it will be exposed to professionals of high caliber and will also showcase what your organization is capable of.

Get featured in industry roundups

Roundups are collections of the best or most happening events in a particular industry. If your content is information based, you have a high chance of featuring in a roundup. Begin by searching for relevant roundups on Google (limit your search to the past month), then pitch your content to the roundup curators. If luck is on your side, the curators will feature your content in their collection. Roundups are searched extensively by business professionals, so your content will reach a niche audience, which works brilliantly for amplification purposes.

Contact people who have shared similar content

While researching for your content, you will surely come across existing articles that have written on the topic similar to yours. Content from reputed sources should already be generating traffic through social media shares. Your best bet is to copy the URL of the article and search for it on sites like Twitter and Facebook. You will be able to spot people who have shared the content, so contact these people through a direct message, requesting them to share what you have done as well.

Link to relevant sites/mention entities when sharing

While researching, you may also come across interesting pieces of information that were quoted by credible sources. It is advisable to link to these sources while writing your article. When you publish your content and promote it on social media, use Twitter mentions or Facebook hashtags to alert those sources that you have used their information. Doing so will increase the chance of your article being viewed by multiple individuals through the mentions.

Use Sniply to leverage the reach of content from more reputed sources

Sniply is a very simple yet effective tool that lets you create a one-line message about your article and display it along with a button prompt. You can use Sniply to overlay your custom message onto any other piece of relevant content. The tool lets you drive conversions from one piece of shared content to another. Let us assume you have found content that shares information about a topic similar to yours; you can use the Sniply tool to add your link to the topic, prompting the reader to delve deeper and gain more knowledge on the subject matter.

Post on relevant LinkedIn groups

LinkedIn is nothing but the Facebook variant for all things professional. If your content has information that can help professionals, LinkedIn is the best platform for promotional purposes. Much like Facebook communities, LinkedIn has an option where you can create groups. Find such groups that could make the most of your content and share it on their pages.

Contact people who have linked to similar content

There is competition everywhere nowadays; you are sure to find a whole lot of articles similar to yours. Some of these articles would have gained immense social share yet may lack certain pieces of information that your article has. You can take advantage of this by pasting the URL of the similar articles on Ahrefs or Open Site Explorers. You will get a list of pages or sites that have used those articles as links. Reach out to those sites and ask them to link your fresher and better content.

Turn content into a PPT/PDF and upload to SlideShare

SlideShare is the perfect place to promote presentations to get the visibility you need. Once you upload your content on SlideShare, you can also share the link on LinkedIn as well. LinkedIn, as we all know, is fast becoming the go-to spot for business professionals when it comes to reading about industry related news and topics.

Leverage the reach of influencers

Reaching out to influencers on a wide scale is a good idea to amplify your content. Getting your content featured by some key influencers or getting them to share your content can amplify your reach drastically. Pick influencers that are relevant to your domain and engage with them. Contact more than one influencer and engage with them regularly for better reach.

The content mentioned above include promotion strategies that are used to their fullest potential by some of the best content marketers on the planet. Of course, some of these strategies may die out while others will evolve. So, to stay ahead of the curve, you'll need to keep your eyes peeled and ears tuned.

How to Rank a One-Page Website

One-page websites are becoming the talk of the town as many companies are switching to these. But what do they mean? Are they search friendly? What should you do to rank them high on Google? You will have all such questions. So, let us take them one by one.

What is a single page website?

A single page website aims to provide minimalist but just enough information for a user to make a decision and act upon it. It has no additional pages and tries to remove all the complexity and varied user journey that a multi-page website would have. A single page website drives the user's attention to the most relevant content. Various real estate companies like Mahindra Lifespaces, Baashyaam Constructions and Ramcons are using this strategy. However, you can have additional pages such as Terms & Conditions page, Privacy Policy, Refunds, Returns & Shipping pages as well as options for alternative languages. These links can be embedded in the footer of the web page.

Pros & cons of a single page website

Pros

1. Mobile responsiveness is better as scrolling works for the mobile phone and the user experience is simple and efficient.

2. You can show the entire journey you want the user to experience through a single page.
3. Controlling the flow of information is easier and you can focus on a particular product or service.
4. You can incorporate a lot of images to make it visually attractive.

Cons

1. Excessive scrolling can be a challenge if there is too much content on a single page.
2. Website speed is an extremely critical factor. Depending on how the site is built, the load time can be longer.
3. Difficult to measure which content section drives visitors to your web page.
4. One-page web pages are not user-friendly for blog-centric companies.
5. Not great for SEO as you only have the possibility of one URL showing up in search results.

How to rank single page website?

- **Content section**

Since it is a one-page website, your content needs to be extraordinary, with a lot of images for the audience to be hooked on to it. However, make sure there is enough content and the readability is not compromised. Also, keep the content updated and fresh, as that is what Google loves. You can keep a navigation bar for various sections on the top so that the visitor can directly jump to that.

- **Exercise DIVs for different content sections**

One of the best practices when it comes to coding for a one-page website is to have separate div for different content sections. It makes the code look organized and neat. These div id names do not directly improve the search engine rank but help indirectly through the anchor tags.

```
<div id="overview">...content...</div>
<div id="amenities">...content...</div>
<div id="gallery">...content...</div>
<div id="floor plan">...content...</div>
```

- **Use anchor links**

Anchor links will help the visitor navigate to a particular portion of the web page. These will create search engine friendly URL on your web page. You can also create anchor text backlinks of your blogs on the site, as below:

```
<div id="overview">...content...</div>
```

//Creating its anchor link

```
<a href= "overview">Overview</a>
```

//backlink example

```
<a href="http://ramcons.in/#amenities">Amenities</a>
```

- **Employ multiple H1 Tags and other on page factors**

Paginate your content using various H1 headers and forms. This technique will control the flow of information and will also act as keywords for your page. Hence, they will help in SEO. You can also look at our detailed blog on the on-page SEO factors that matter to see how you can employ some of these techniques for your web page.

- **Encourage linking to social media**

Social media does matter for SEO and hence it is a good idea to link to various social media platforms so that you can reach out to a larger audience for online marketing. You can also implement various other link building methods, which are listed on our blog.

Some additional interesting facts

Bounce rates could be high for a single page website because Google Analytics will not account for numerous page views unless you refresh the page.

Single page websites may not be useful for every business, but they are quite appealing and create unique user experience altogether. You can use such tricks to rank your page higher.

Ultimate Checklist for On-Page and Off-Page SEO

Creating a blog has become very important for every business. The actual challenge, though, comes when you are faced with the Herculean task of making your post pop-up on the top page of all leading Search Engine Result Pages (SERPs). Search Engine Optimization (SEO) plays a pivotal role in spiking your web page's ranking and making sure it receives the exposure it truly deserves. Read on for some foolproof techniques to optimize your page and drive all your targeted traffic right to it.

On-Page Checklist

Here is a list of On-Page Factors that matters the most:

Title Tag

As per Google's algorithm, the length of the title tag should be 55 to 60 characters. If it crosses this limit, only the first 60 characters will show up in the SERPs. So, ensure that the title is crisp and conveys everything it needs to in the first 60 characters itself.

Meta Description

Meta descriptions are often used to give us a brief explanation of the blog post. Make sure you include all the necessary keywords in the description. The length of the Meta description is limited to 155 to 160 characters. Similar to the title tag, even if the length of the Meta description crosses 160, only the first 160 characters will show up in the SERPs.

URL Length

Google identifies web pages mainly by the URL and the title. So, to rank higher on Google, you need to use your focus keywords on your URL. Additionally, try making your URL as short and sweet as possible. Unless your post is an event-based blog, avoid mentioning the year in your URL as Google tends to categorize it as outdated content. This, in turn, decreases your ranking.

Heading (H1)

The heading of your blog post needs to be in the H1 tag and should contain the exact keyword match. This helps Googlebot in ranking your post as high as possible in SERPs.

Sub-headings (H2)

The sub-headings of your blog post need to be in the H2 tag. If you are focusing on more than one set of keywords in your post, use the other keywords in your sub-headings for better SERP ranking.

Use LSI keywords in the body and headings

Once you have completed your Keyword Research, perform a Google search for those keywords. This will give you a set of keywords, under the top results, titled "Searches related to." These keywords are called Latent Semantic Indexing (LSI) keywords and are the most frequently used keywords by visitors. Using these keywords in your content and heading will rank your post better.

Keyword density

Keyword density is the number of times your focus keyword has been used in your content. A high-ranking post should primarily have a keyword density of 1.5% based on its length.

Use Multimedia (Image, Video and Infographics)

All Digital Marketers know that Content Is King. It keeps the visitors engaged in the post and has the potential to make a post go viral. To keep your visitors glued to your blog, make sure you give out more information in a lesser span of time. Images, videos and infographics are your best bet, as they help in better understanding of the content.

Alt tag

The images in your blog post play a vital role in ranking your page as well. Insert the keywords in the alt-text used to describe the images to make them show up on Google searches and, in turn, rank your page higher on Google.

Use keywords in first two lines (within 100 words)

Apart from the fact that your keywords need to be frequently used in your post, the placement of the keywords is also important for better SEO. Use your keywords in first 100 words of your content for higher SERP ranking.

Use Outbound Links

Outbound links give Google a better understanding of your content based on the links provided to other web pages.

Use Internal Links

Internal links help in keeping your users engaged in the blog by providing old links related to the current article within the same website.

Content Is King

Quality and quantity are both important for good content. A blog post without any one of these will not help in keeping users engaged, which will lead to a decrease in SERP ranking over the course of time. To understand this concept better, let us take the example of Alice and Bob. Alice's blog is ranked in the first position, but her content lacks quality whereas Bob's blog is currently ranked in the 4th position, but his content keeps his users engaged for a long time. Google will analyze this behavior and automatically rank Bob's blog higher than Alice's due to better content.

HTTPS for domain

Using HTTPS for your blog will make it secured. It also helps in increasing your visitors' confidence and trust in your content.

Responsive Design

As per the latest Google algorithm, a web page needs to have a good responsive design, to adapt to all platforms such as mobiles and tablets.

Site Speed

The speed at which a web page loads fully is of paramount importance. Site speed should not be compromised by data speed. You could have the latest website design, but if your site does not load quickly, you will lose you customer then and there. So improving your sites page speed should be of utmost importance.

Robots.txt

Robots. txt helps to block unwanted information in the web page.

XML sitemap

When Google indexes the page, it can be seen in the XML sitemap through the following links:

- domain.com/sitemap.xml
- domain.com/sitemap_index.xml

On-page Grader

The on-page grader is a Moz tool to ensure your web page is optimized. It gives you a closer insight into the things, which need to be done to get a grade A web page. The tool focuses on the following factors to get a higher SERP ranking.

- Checks the accessibility to search engines
- Avoids keyword stuffing in document
- Avoids keyword stuffing in page title
- Avoids multiple page title elements
- Checks broad keyword usage in page title
- Checks if the exact keyword is used in the document text at least once
- Checks only one canonical URL
- Checks for sufficient characters in content
- Checks for sufficient words in content
- Checks if the exact keyword is used in page title
- Checks if the keyword is at the beginning of page title
- Checks for keywords in image alt attribute
- Checks keywords in the Meta description
- Checks optimal page title length
- Checks optimal use of keywords in H1 tags
- Checks if URL uses only standard characters
- Checks if external links are used
- Checks if keywords are used in your URL
- Checks the meta descriptions
- Use Static URLs

- Avoids keyword stuffing in the URL
- Avoids too many external links
- Avoids too many internal links
- Includes a rel canonical tag
- Minimizes URL length
- Only one meta description
- Optimal meta description length

Structured Data Error

Structured data error is a webmaster error. Fixing this error is also one of the effective ways of optimizing your website. Though this is not a ranking factor, it helps in eradicating all errors on the website.

Mobile Usability Error

Fixing the mobile usability error is of utmost importance as the Google Penguin update gives more priority to mobile devices and most of the traffic driven to a website is through mobile. Fixing this error addresses the following concerns:

- Clickable elements too close
- Content wider than screen
- Viewport not set
- Text too small to read

Html Improvements

These errors can be found under the "HTML improvements" tag in "Search Console." These errors pop-up when the title and meta description are missing and a duplicate title and meta description is placed on the web page.

Off-Page Checklist

Local Listing

Listing your business with Google is a great way to ensure that people can see you on the internet. This helps with local SEO and when we build backlinks in specific regional listings, Google will understand which region is targeted.

Social Bookmarking

Social bookmarking sites are the best way to promote any website, event or brand in a shorter span of time. Marking a link to social bookmarking sites plays a very effective role in creating traffic and getting higher ranking in SERPs.

Some of the most popular social bookmarking sites are StumbleUpon; Scoop it, Reddit, Youmob, Pearltrees and Savenkeep to name a few.

Image Submission

Image sharing sites help in improving your website traffic. If you are optimizing your content, then it's only for the web search. But nowadays image search is also improving, so people have begun to submit their images to image sharing sites. Mentioned below are a few good high PR image sharing sites, which will help you improve backlinking through images:

- Instagram
- Flickr
- Pinterest
- Tumblr

Audio Submission

Uploading audio files is another prime SEO activity which is useful in promoting your website. You can backlink these files to high PR audio sharing websites for effective SEO. Few of the audio sharing websites are mentioned below:

- SoundCloud
- Podbean
- Podmatic
- Mobypicture

Video Submission

Video submission is one of the most prominent and powerful methods of promoting a website. While uploading a relevant video, make sure the title and description contain the focus keyword for better ranking. A few examples of video submission sites are:

- Myspace
- Flickr
- Dailymotion
- Vimeo

Web 2.0

You can create a blog and directly post it on high PR Web 2.0 sites. Getting natural backlinks is one of the key SEO strategies to increase traffic and, eventually, the ranking of a website or blog. There are many sources of natural backlinks, which are favored by Google. They include High Pagerank Dofollow web 2.0 websites, such as:

- Blogger
- Weebly
- WordPress
- Hubpages

Profile Creation Sites

Profile linking websites have improved the level of engagement of users. They offer much better distinctiveness and enable the visitors to interact with the website in an easier manner. Profile creation is a method, which offers a brand new strategy to SEO professionals for the best SEO services and link building services. They also significantly provide a more substantial perspective to present creativeness as well as improve the interaction standard of audiences. It is extremely simple to make a "Dofollow" profile backlink.

Classified Submission

High PR classified submission sites are an easier way to generate leads and promote your products online. Classified submission sites are very effective for link building, boosting the ranking in search engines and generating more leads for your business.

PPT Submission

There are lots of benefits in using PPT sharing sites. You can easily share your PDF files online on these high PR PPT submission websites. These highly authoritative PPT Sharing and submission sites are frequently updated on a regular and daily basis. That's why search engines like to crawl these sites more often. Getting dofollow backlinks from PPT submission sites will get your targeted keywords optimized, and it will help in increasing your site visibility in search engines.

Participate on Quora

Quora is a great way to drive traffic and get backlinks to your blog. The Quora community consists of an incredibly large number of users discussing a wide variety of subjects and topics. If you have not yet, then you should join Quora right away and start participating in discussions. You can start replying to questions and mention a post of your blog or the homepage of your blog, as long as it is relevant to the question.

SEO techniques are changing constantly; however, this on-page and off-page SEO checklist will help you stay ahead in the game.

9 Ways to Leverage Local SEO and Google Maps for Your Business

When it comes to Search Engine Optimization (SEO) and digital marketing for your business, one must pay attention to things beyond just their own website, especially if you own a local business. In the past couple of years, digital marketers have gradually understood the importance of strong online marketing efforts that include local SEO and Google Maps (or Google My Business) as well.

If you think it's enough to just optimize your website to perfection, then you are on the wrong path. Since July 2014, Google uses an algorithm called Pigeon. This is one of Google's local search algorithm updates. The aim of this algorithm is to increase the ranking of local listings in a search.

The changes in the ranking made by this algorithm are also shown in the Google Maps results. In other terms, when a person searches for a particular kind of business in a locality, the results will be based on user location and the listing available in the local directory.

For example, if you are searching for spas in Chennai on Google, the search result will be like this:

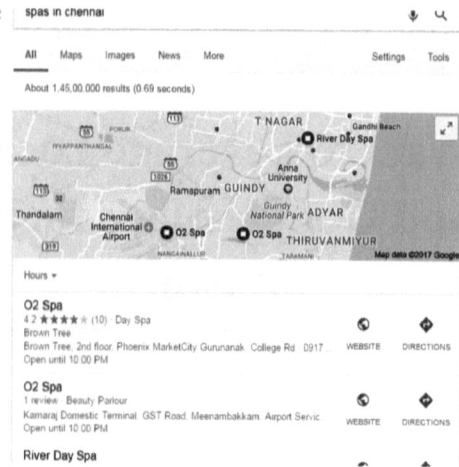

Even before the pages are ranked, there will be three map listings. The map listing will also have a toggle button – 'More Places' that allows you to check for more map listings. Similarly, another search result for 'Bakeries in Egmore' shows this result:

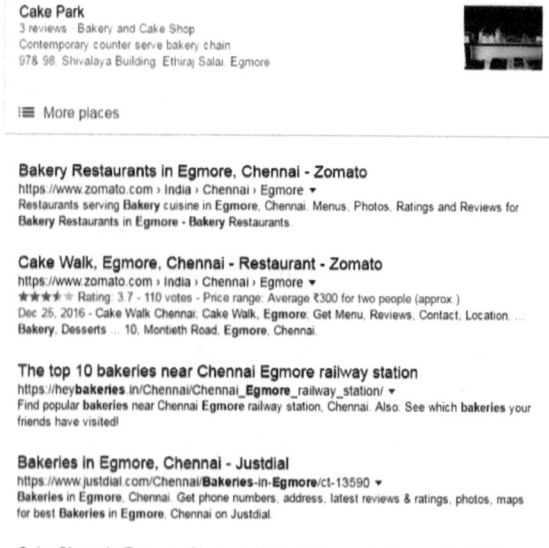

When a person searches for 'bakeries, Egmore' in the query box, he gets a result where there are three map listings and 5+ organic listings. So, even if you have the best website, it might be at the eighth or ninth position. How many users would scroll down all the way through eight or more entries to click on the actual website?

The number of people who would reach until the end of the page will definitely be way less than the ones who click directly on the map listing or any organic listing. Hence, you must constantly watch these listings and optimize your presence in the map and directory sites. The 3-pack map listings by Google can be a marketing game-changer for your business, for they have a highly valuable exposure, thus generating quality traffic and new customers.

Here are some of the best practices that you must follow to implement a successful Google Maps marketing and local SEO strategy:

It is important to maintain a physical address for your business

No matter whether your business is B2B or B2C, it is important to maintain a local address for your company. This is important to rank in the Google local 3-pack map listing. Also, having a local address is an important search engine factor for local SEO. Google has reported that there is an increase in queries containing "near me" – for example, restaurants near me or salons near me. The distance from the location of the user is critical in these searches.

Set up and maintain a Google My Business Account

Your Google My Business (GMB) account plays a major role in Google Maps Marketing and local SEO. In fact, your GMB determines and has an effect on your online presence in Google Maps, Search, and G+.

Google My Business offers a simple and easy way for you to create a listing for your business. You can also claim an existing one. You must just make sure that all the information listed in your GMB page is accurate and complete. It also gives you the ability to put up pictures of your business or a 360-degree view of your interiors. It's also important to choose the most appropriate category to list your business. This can have a direct impact on what kind searches you show up on. What's more? GMB is free.

Concentrate on your business NAP

Your business NAP – Name, address and phone number, should be consistent in both your GMB page as well as on your website. Also, make sure that your business NAP appears exactly the same across the web on third-party websites, directory listings and social media profiles. These citations, i.e. your company's NAP in other websites and listings determine the legitimacy of your business and it's beneficial if your NAP is available in various websites.

Have a separate web page for each of your products or services

Your business might have multiple products or services. Dedicating a separate web page for each and every type of product and service can help in optimizing every page. In other words, instead of over-optimizing a single page with a lot of keywords, you can optimize each page of your website with the relevant set of keywords around a theme. It doesn't mean you need to have a page for every keyword, but make sure each type of product/service and each service area (i.e. locations) are covered.

Create mindful citations

Be it a citation in Zomato for your business or a mention on another website, you must make sure that the mentions are made sensibly. If you can build citations in trustworthy websites and good listing directories, you can increase the value of your local SEO significantly.

Some of the things that you need to keep in mind while creating or building citations are:

- Make sure that any citation about your business is 100% accurate, especially the NAP.
- Remove or place a request to remove any duplicate listings in listing directories.
- Try to build mentions in websites that are relevant to your industries.

Work towards generating Google Reviews (positive ones, of course)

Reviews in Google Places are a crucial ranking factor for the search engine. Having good reviews in Google will definitely assist you in being listed in the Google 3-pack map listings. You can ask your customers to leave a review. Alternatively, you can also offer incentives or discounts on the next purchase for customers who review your service or product on Google. Even reviews from social media channels are now displayed on Google.

Embed Google Maps on your site

Last but not least – embed the Google Map of your business location on your website in the "contact us" page. This technique is a proven way to boost the SEO value of your website. This needs to be combined with local schema to give Google complete visibility on what kind of business is being run.

Many business owners have found Google Maps and Local SEO marketing to be intensely helpful and beneficial for their businesses. Have you started applying these best practices?

Make sure your website and blog are super-fast

In recent times, there has been a lot of talk on website speed and implementation of AMP (Accelerated Mobile Pages) to ensure that experience on mobile and desktop is fantastic. This is critical even for a local business because blog content focused on your city or location of business can be crucial in attracting the right audience. For example, one of our most popular blogs is on marketing events in Bangalore and we created this to target marketing professionals in the city when we first launched our services there.

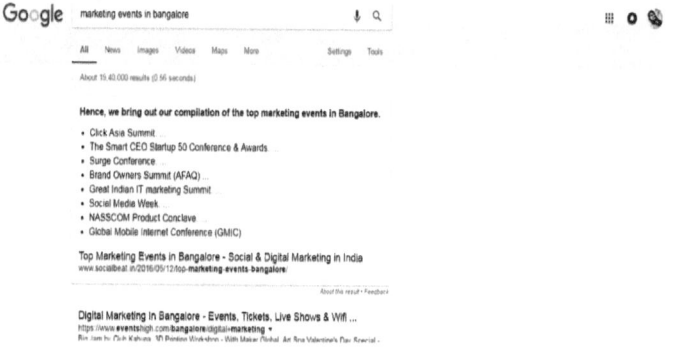

Build a brand

Google and other search engines are starting to reward content that is customized to users (in this case, content can be customized to a local audience) and they continue to show preference for sites and brands that users already know of. Hence, it is critical to keep track of how many users are searching for your brand (Google Analytics and Google Search Console can help with that) and not just for the product and service that you are offering.

Videos

How to Create Low Cost Videos to Tell Your Brand Story

Who does not love a good story? We humans are inherently suckers for good stories. They make us feel happy, sad, motivated, joyous, angry and various other emotions.

There is a reason why we spend hours binge-watching series, or why we watch movies or bury ourselves in books. All of these mediums have one thing in common – stories! It is all around us.

Storytelling is a very powerful communication tool and is probably the best way to build a brand. Brands that have made a mark and stand apart today have been successful in telling their stories in a unique manner. There is also an art to storytelling and when done right it can help you get exceptionally good results!

We are all aware of the classic ways of storytelling through words and images. Today, however, the trend has shifted towards videos. This holds true especially when applied to digital marketing. Videos are more powerful than simple imagery and are super illustrative; they are also easily memorable and allow creating a stronger bond between the brand and the audience.

Videos in digital marketing can prove to be extremely powerful and worthwhile for both brands and consumers. A lot of effort goes into conceptualizing and producing a video and it can prove to be quite costly. However, today, there are a lot of ways in which you can create good quality videos with a low budget.

Opt for short videos to convey your message

Short videos go well with our hectic lives and concise attention spans. Also, 70% of the smartphone users are consuming content via their mobile devices while they are on the go. Thus, the crisper and briefer the content, the better it is. YouTube is not the only video-embracing platform available online. There is no dearth of video-centric platforms and 90% of these platforms are famous for hosting short-form videos. Instagram and many other channels today host videos, including Facebook and Twitter. The world's first Instagram trailer was released back in 2013 for the movie *Jobs,* which was a fifteen-second packed video with dramatic music and slow-motion shots of Ashton Kutcher reciting inspiring dialogs about eccentric, misfit rebels. It is almost like the first full theatrical trailer for the movie, except shorter.

Creating short-form videos is all about how creative you can get in less than a minute. These videos are streamed to viewers on a range of platforms that increase the reach exponentially. They are also far more successful and have a wider reach because they are "snackable" in nature, easier to consume and producing them costs far less than creating a long video.

Smartphones are the best chattels

It's not necessary to film a video with the help of high-end equipment and lights. Your best asset is in your pocket – your smartphone. As a brand, it might come across as a ridiculous idea, but it actually is a very cost-effective and quick way of creating videos. It is not necessary to get engulfed in creating huge budget videos. You can convey your story through an excellent video shot on your smartphone or tablet (of course with a good quality camera).

Your script is paramount

The script plays a huge role in the video as well. The content should be clear and precise with no ambiguity. The video holds no power if the visuals are perfect and the content is lacking. Both are of great importance. Thus, make sure you get your script right first. If you choose to outsource the production of a video inclusive of the conceptualization, it will cost you a substantial amount of money. However, if you decide to prepare the script beforehand then it might save you time and money. There are also affordable marketplaces from where you can subcontract video productions and these come at a remarkably low-cost.

Affordable online marketplaces

The Internet is a great place to find the solution for your woes and this case is no different. There are some really affordable marketplaces like Fiverr.com, which has professionals from all over the world who can help create the video of your choice at really affordable prices, starting from $5. All you have to do is describe how you want your video to be and they will get it done for you within a matter of 24–48 hours. The system is commendable and you get what you seek, at really good rates.

DIY Videos

If you do not wish to outsource your videos, there is also an option to create your own videos with readily available online tools. Even beginners can create videos like a pro! Examples of such websites include: VideoScribe, Animoto, Sparkol, etc. With Videoscribe and Sparkol, you can create amazing whiteboard-style animation videos. Animoto is ideal for those who are looking for a really simple way to create a video. All you need to do is select images and upload them with soundtracks provided by the tool.

With these tips, you can surely make the right impression with your videos. To make an amazing video all you need is an idea, a good script and the right tools. Gone are the days when we had to buy expensive video equipment! With the development of technology, you can create the perfect video for your brand at an affordable rate!

App Marketing

A Beginner's Guide to App Marketing

There is an app for everything these days. If you are a heavy user, you probably have numerous apps installed on your smartphone. Each app in your phone serves a purpose, giving you a good reason to use when required. The only thing is, there are too many apps that share similar features and functionality, so you need to come up with ingenious ways to make your app stand out.

At present, there are more than 4 million apps in Google's Play Store and Apple's App Store combined and these numbers are increasing at a huge rate. To stand out in this overflowing marketplace, your app needs powerful marketing and promotion. Here is a quick guide on the many ways you can market your newly launched mobile app:

Optimize your app for app stores

Even before you begin marketing your app, you need to be 100% sure it is prepped and ready for displaying on a selected app store. Little things like the app icon, software updates and app descriptions play a big role in your app's awareness and life cycle in a store. Keep a cheat sheet for app store optimization next to you throughout the development and marketing of your app.

Create a landing page

A lot of apps launching today are really just an extension of a product or service that already has a strong presence on the web. If you are going the reverse way, you still need some sort of website presence that can be used as a promotive platform. The best option is a landing page, which can be used to promote your app organically. Let us say you are writing an informative blog article that centers around your app-based product or people search for the product you offer on Google. If the first point of communication is a landing page, there is a big chance that searchers get converted into a user of your app.

Make the most you can of the freedom of expression offered on the landing page. You can provide detailed information about your product and even create a mock version of your app to give users a taste of what to expect.

Human, a fitness initiative, launched as an app to inspire people of all ages to get active for a minimum of 30 minutes every day. To boost awareness of the app, a landing page was created that explained in detail the various features and benefits of using the app. The landing page included app screenshots, a simulator that showed real-time statistics of the app's usage and various testimonials. Installs of Human hit the 1 million mark and the app was also rated amongst the best of 2014.

Utilize paid promotions – App install ads

Advertising is the fastest way to create awareness about a product and the same can be said for your app. Many third-party services enable you to create and promote app install ads. So keep your finances in check and work out the best possible deals for advertising your app.

Facebook and Google's app install campaigns are the best to start with. Here are the steps:

- Create a campaign with relevant targets such as location, audience and budget

- Design ad copy creatives with a unique selling proposition
- For Google search, choose relevant keywords that the target audience would normally search for
- Launch the campaign
- Measure the results with important metrics and optimize accordingly

Get social

If shelling out money for advertising is not a good option for you, try the alternative route with social media promotions. Blogging, hashtagging and page posts are some of the many techniques you can utilize on social media. Audience engagement helps build trust and value for your app and works wonders in the long run, provided you have patience and perseverance when using this marketing method.

Request for app ratings and reviews

One of the quickest ways to increase app installs is to request current users to write reviews and rate your app. App Store algorithms calculate app popularity through user reviews and number of downloads, which ultimately push your app to the Top Charts. You can implement the review and rating feature in your app via a number of unique ways; asking for reviews after multiple usages of the app or providing additional app features after a review or rating is done.

Install mobile app tracking

Just like Google's numerous tools that help keep track of a website's performance or the number of views and clicks on an ad, Mobile App Tracking tools help you track the number of times your app is installed. Even when you promote your app through paid advertising, you can use app tracker tools to see from which method of promotion your app is benefiting the most. Doing so helps in managing your ad expenses as well as gives you some pointers on what needs to change to enhance your app's user experience.

App Store Optimization Cheat Sheet

So, you have developed a mobile app, excellent, but what next?

There are more than 4 million apps in the Google Play Store and Apple App Store and this number will only increase in the coming years. While each app is exclusive to the developer, only a few get the deserved recognition from users. To be precise, the fate of your app after its development depends on how many users download and use it. According to research, 63% of apps are discovered through app store searches, so it is highly essential to optimize your app for the app store.

Here are some best practices to get more app download and to increase your rankings in the app store:

The app's name should be creative and informative

No, naming your app after you or your business will not work well. A good idea would be to choose two to three keywords and using at least one of them in the title of your app. According to data, apps with keywords in the title rank 10.3% higher than those without a keyword in the title. This way, your app will show easily in the search results. However, make sure that you do not make the app name look like spam by overstuffing it with keywords. The title needs to be short because that is what users can read in a single screen. Obviously, you do not want your title to get cut. Titles are usually cut after the 23rd character (including spaces) in the app store and the 30th character in Google Play. The first thing that the users see about your app is the name and icon. This is the first and the best chance to impress your users. Therefore, be cautious and creative when thinking of a name for your app.

Always include a description

Most of the times, users may need an app for some particular function, but they may not be sure which app to download for the same. In such cases, the description option in the app store comes in handy. Reading the description of the app will help the users know what your app does and it will also decrease the chances of uninstalls as the users know about the app well before downloading it.

Make sure the description is precise, concise and brings out what the app does exactly. Use bullet points wherever required and avoid dense paragraphs.

Have an original app icon

As we said before, an app icon and the app's name are the ones that catch your user's eyes easily. Make sure that your app's icon is designed from scratch. Also, do not make it too elaborate or complicated. Keep it simple, unique as well as attractive and make sure the icon breaks through the clutter. Do remember that the Play Store and the App Store have varying standards in terms of size, geometry and color scheme of app icons, so design the icons accordingly. The iOS icons should be sized to at least 1024 × 1024 pixels and Google Play requires a 512 × 512 icon.

Use screenshots tactfully

Have you noticed those screenshots that are shown in the app store when you check out an app? Well, that is your next chance to capture the attention of your potential app users. To make a visitor download your app, you must place screenshots tactfully in this section. You can upload up to five screenshots for an iOS app and eight for an Android one. However, only two or three screenshots will appear in the gallery when the page loads. Only use screenshots that will differentiate your app from other similar apps. For the best results, you could A/B test various screenshots to see which drives the most downloads.

Update your app regularly

Like any other software, your mobile apps will also need regular updates and upgrades. If you launch your app and forget it, your users will download it and forget or uninstall it. Release periodical updates with relevant release notes explaining what's new in the update.

Encourage your users to review and rate you

You do not have to urge them to review or rate you with pop-ups every other minute, but gently nudge your users to rate your app. This will always help in increasing your views. Furthermore, do not ignore negative reviews, pay attention to what was wrong in the users' experience, and try to fix it. The apps with high ratings are all ones that keep their audience engaged and take customer feedback positively. You can also make use of influencer marketing to get your app reviewed by top digital influencers.

Price it right

If your app is something that needs to be bought, set a competitive pricing. Instead of making your app more expensive than other similar apps, set a nominal price and improvise on making your app the best in the category. If your app is free, then add it to the in-app purchases category to improve its listing and visibility.

Make your app language and device compatible

When your app is available in various languages and is compatible with different OS versions, it is bound to get more views and reach than an app released only for one OS and in English. Both the iOS and the Play Store allow you to localize your listings to make discovering your app easier for customers in other countries.

We hope you have understood the various best practices that must be followed to improve your app downloads.

About Social Beat

Founded in 2012, Social Beat is one of India's leading digital marketing solutions company, enabling businesses to build their brands and achieve business results via the digital medium.

Social Beat is a Premier Google Partner, recommended Facebook agency, a member of Facebook India SME Council and a trusted online expert with offices in Bangalore, Chennai & Mumbai. Our expertise with video content, as well as platforms such as Influencer and 22 Languages, makes us the ideal digital marketing solutions partner for brands and businesses as they seek to engage with audiences in both urban and rural markets. Our 90-member team of digital experts offers integrated digital marketing solutions including UX, web development, social media marketing, content marketing, video production, search engine optimisation, digital advertising, influencer marketing and impactful language content.

In 2017, Social Beat bagged two awards at the Social Samosa "Best Social Media Brands" and was the only agency recognised by Google India for innovation in both, Search & Display Advertising.

With focus verticals of real estate, retail, FMCG and BFSI, Social Beat has over 200 clients including TVS Motors, Mahindra Lifespaces, CavinKare, Murugappa Group, Sterling Holidays, House of Hiranandani, Brigade Group, Forum Mall, Specsmakers, Chola Finance, Casagrand, FundsIndia, Klay Schools, Mphasis, Dr. Mohan's Diabetes Specialities Centre, Motherhood and TVS Logistics amongst many others.

www.ingramcontent.com/pod-product-compliance
Lightning Source LLC
Chambersburg PA
CBHW020743180526
45163CB00001B/329